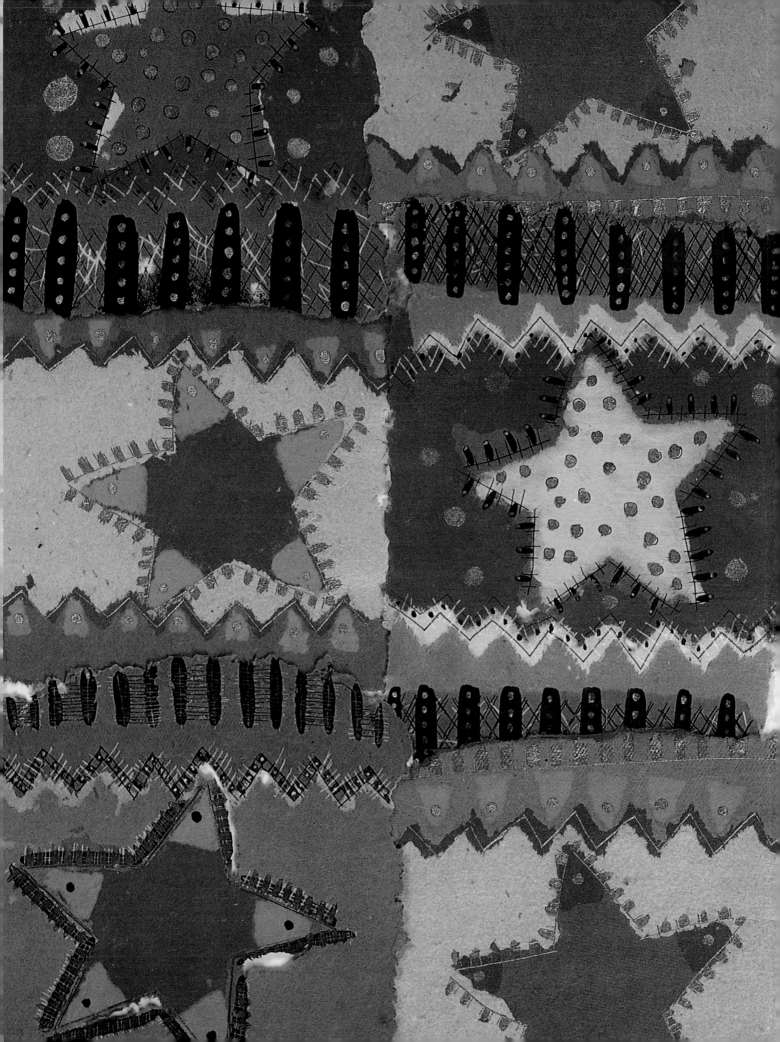

*The* DK *Art School*

# AN INTRODUCTION TO MIXED MEDIA

## MICHAEL WRIGHT

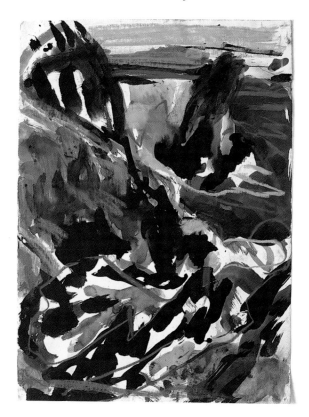

**DORLING KINDERSLEY**
LONDON • NEW YORK • STUTTGART
IN ASSOCIATION WITH THE ROYAL ACADEMY OF ARTS

# A DORLING KINDERSLEY BOOK

**Art editor** Tassy King
**Project editor** Joanna Warwick
**Assistant editor** Neil Lockley
**Design assistant** Stephen Croucher
**Senior editor** Gwen Edmonds
**Senior art editor** Claire Legemah
**Managing editor** Sean Moore
**Managing art editor** Toni Kay
**US editors** Julee Binder, Constance Mersel
**Production controller** Meryl Silbert
**Photography** Steve Gorton
**Picture research** Jo Walton

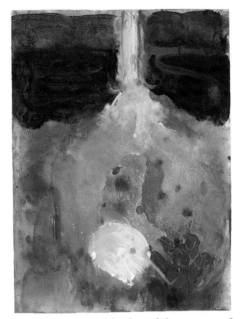

To the memory of my father, John, and for the unfailing support of my mother, Mary, and uncle, Michael, who have encouraged my artistic endeavors since early childhood.

First American Edition, 1995
2 4 6 8 10 9 7 5 3 1

Published in the United States by
Dorling Kindersley Publishing Inc, 95 Madison Avenue
New York, New York 10016

Library of Congress Cataloging-in-Publication Data

Wright, Michael, 1955–
  An Introduction to Mixed Media/Michael Wright -- 1st American ed.
    p.  cm. -- (The DK Art School)
Includes index.
ISBN 0-7894-0000-6
1.  Mixed Media painting -- Technique.  I. Title.  II. Series.
ND1505.W75  1995
760--dc20                                          84-48533
                                                         CIP

Color reproduction by Colourscan in Singapore
Printed and bound by Toppan in Singapore

# CONTENTS

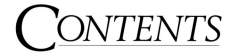

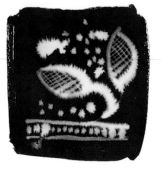

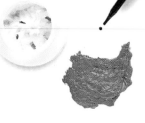

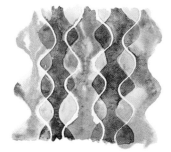

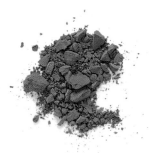

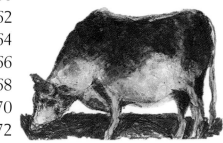

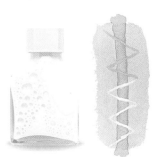

# MIXED MEDIA

THE TERM "MIXED MEDIA" is commonly used
to define works of art that combine
different painting and drawing media. It is
an exciting and experimental working practice
that allows for the combination of likely and
unlikely media. As a result it has allowed for the
extension of drawing and painting techniques into
areas of photography, printmaking, collage, and bas-
relief construction. Combining different media has become
a consistent feature of contemporary practice, and it is rare to
see a group exhibition now in which there is not some use of
mixed media. Most visual arts courses encourage students to
focus on the use of mixed media to develop a more imaginative
approach to image making
and to learn more about
materials. Mixing your media
is an excellent way to revitalize your awareness
of a familiar medium and to establish new and
imaginative interpretations on familiar themes.

*Charcoal, pastel
and ink*

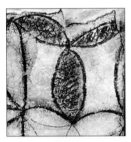
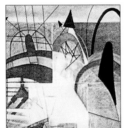

*These are mixed media studies in which the artist has combined
drawing media with collage materials.*

## Combining your materials

When developing a watercolor, it is usual to lightly
sketch in pencil, then work on the image in watercolor
washes, and finish by adding highlights in an opaque
gouache medium. Similarly, when creating a pastel
painting, charcoal is often used to establish the basic
drawing, which is then overworked in pastel.

The development of mixed
media as a technique has been
encouraged by the relaxed
attitude toward experimentation
that has arisen in this century.
The advent of new art materials,
such as acrylics, and the
development of new creative
techniques in collage, print,
and photographic processes
has seen an increase in mixed
media works not just in
painting, but in all the visual

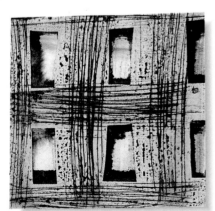

*This striking tonal composition was developed using
a wax resist technique. Warm liquid wax was applied
to mask areas of the paper and to resist the ink.*

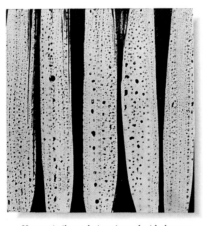

*Here a similar technique is used with the wax
painted in vertical bands down a sheet of paper.
Black ink was then brushed across the surface.*

arts – graphics, illustration, and textiles. Looking at the breadth of materials used in combination in this century, it is exciting to realize that the expressive range of media for mixing appears to be inexhaustible. The beauty and success of many mixed media works is due to the artist's capacity for combining different media within an esthetically pleasing composition, and in the hands of an experienced artist, mundane materials such as newsprint, sandpaper, and wax crayons become vehicles of eloquent expression.

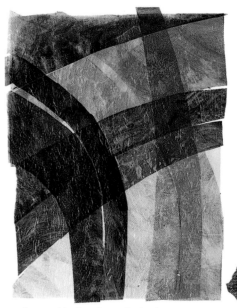

*A composition based on arches has been constructed using collage. Sheets of colored tissue paper have been cut and laminated between layers of diluted PVA glue and the colors optically mixed to create new colors.*

### Getting started

Most of the effects and methods which will be described in the coming pages are unique to mixed media. You will be encouraged to exploit the particular qualities of different media by using them in new contexts of either juxtaposition or layering. You will be guided through the basic principles of drawing, painting, collaging, and printing, using the common range of materials carried by most art shops, alongside materials found in the home. Finally, you will experiment with less common materials and techniques.

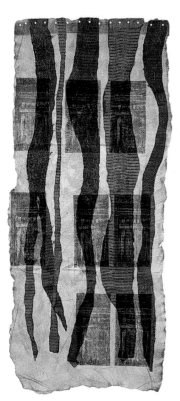

*This print was developed using a monotype process. The brown strips were printed on corrugated paper and then laminated between sheets of tissue paper.*

*A collage of found and cut wooden shapes has been painted using a combination of painting techniques.*

7

# A BRIEF HISTORY

MIXED MEDIA IS USUALLY REGARDED as an art form peculiar to the 20th century. However, throughout the history of painting, works have been produced that have successfully combined a range of the usual and more unlikely materials. There are also particular phases in Western art when mixed media works were created by using materials such as gold leaf in combination with other drawing and painting media.

FROM EARLIEST TIMES artists have created mixed media compositions by combining materials such as charcoal with earth colors and extracted minerals, such as oxides or vegetable dyes. The preparation of the ground, which is the surface to which the pigment is applied, has also led to a great deal of experimentation with materials. Artists have worked on wood, velum, and various natural fibers that have been pressed or woven into papers and textiles, and also on glass and metals such as copperplate or gold leaf.

**Illuminated manuscripts and icons**
Early Italian church paintings are prime examples of the beauty of combining media. Artists used underpainting and combined areas of luminous pigments and gold leaf. The splendor of the gold leaf was often heightened by a technique of embossing the gesso ground, burnishing the gold leaf and, occasionally, by the addition of precious gems. These works were created using the richest materials available. They aimed to transport the viewer from the temporal world into a state of meditation on the nature of the divine. During the 16th century, artists used sanguine (a deep blood red) earth color, with additional highlights in white chalk on colored paper, to evoke the skin

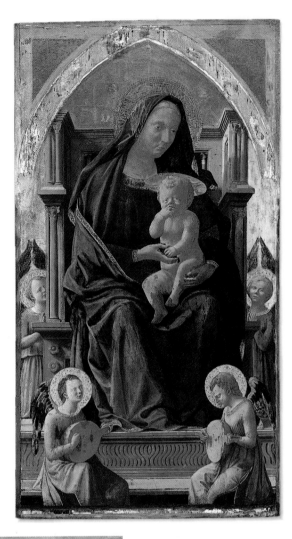

**Tomasso Masaccio, *Virgin and Child,* 1426,**
*53 x 29½ in (135 x 75 cm)*
*Masaccio (1401–28) made a remarkable contribution to the development of Western art through the assimilation of perspective within the picture space of his compositions. The charm of this painting resides in a unique combination of treatment and materials. The use of the paint to create a naturalistic illusion of form contrasts with the abstract symbolism, the hierarchical arrangement of the figures, and the use of gold leaf in the halos.*

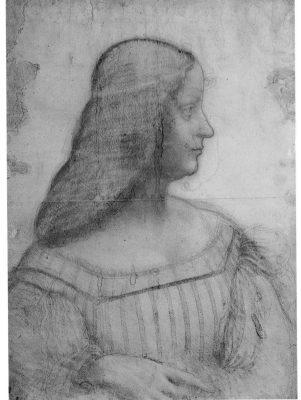

**Leornado Da Vinci, *Isabella d'Este,* 1500**
*25 x 18 in (63 x 46 cm)*
*Leonardo da Vinci (1452–1519) was the archetypal Renaissance man who experimented with new approaches and materials. Leonardo was also instrumental in developing the practice of combining pastel with other drawing media. The term pastel is derived from the word "pasta," which means paste. It refers to the method of manufacture where pure pigment and chalks are mixed into a paste with a binding solution of gum and allowed to dry into crayons. In this eloquent profile of Isabella d'Este, the work has been developed in black chalk, with additional highlights visible in the use of a yellow pastel to add color to the neckline of the dress.*

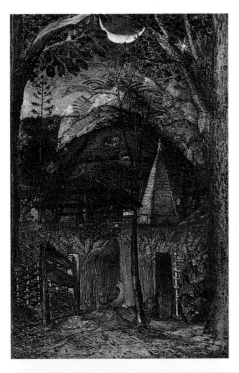

tones of the figure and to create warm and cool sensations of light and shadow. In 17th-century Holland, it became fashionable to heighten drawings, mainly of landscape scenes, with a limited range of tones using yellow, brown, rose madder, green, and blue watercolors. The mixed media technique of creating tinted drawings was further developed in Britain by a number of major artists, including Turner (1775–1851),

**Samuel Palmer, *A Hilly Scene,* 1826,**
*8 x 5¼ in (20.5 x 13.5 cm)*
*In this visionary evocation of an idealized rustic scene, Palmer (1805–81) has loaded the painting with symbolism. Pigments mixed with gum arabic create varying areas of luminous washes and opaque color which adds to the substance of the linear drawing in pen and ink.*

who lifted watercolor from the status of minor studies to complete compositions on paper, that were accepted as works in their own right. Two other major British artists, William Blake (1757–1827) and his pupil Samuel Palmer, experimented with watercolor in combination with other media to create innovative mixed media works. Blake applied colored washes to his prints and along with Palmer, combined watercolor with tempera and gum to build up complex surfaces combining pen and ink with transparent and opaque layers of watercolor.

## Ninteenth-century artists

An outstanding 19th-century exponent of mixed media techniques was Edgar Degas, who combined pastel with charcoal, distemper, and monotype printing techniques. Degas deliberately exploited visual tension by contrasting the varying surface qualities of the mixed media.

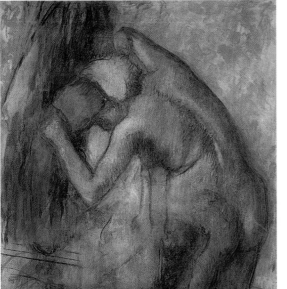

**Edgar Degas, *Woman Arranging Her Hair,* 1895–1900,**
*30½ x 29½ in (77 x 75 cm)*
*Toward the end of his long career, and with the failing of his eyesight, Degas worked increasingly in pastels, which he combined with charcoal, distemper paint, and monotype printing inks. He was preoccupied with the subject of the body in motion and would overlay a tonal composition in charcoal with pastels.*

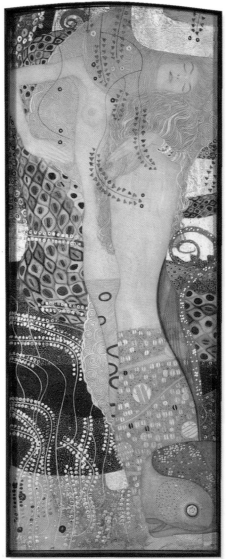

## Adding color

There are many examples of artists who add color in a transparent or opaque form to linear drawings, using either watercolor or gouache. The sculptor August Rodin and the painters Vincent Van Gogh, Gustav Klimt, and Egon Schiele were all skilled exponents of mixed media techniques. The work of Klimt emerged out of the stylistic development of Art Nouveau, and many works combine oil paint with gold leaf in a technique that evokes the religious works of previous centuries.

**Gustav Klimt, *Watersnakes,* 1904–07,**
*19¾ x 8 in (50 x 20 cm)*
*Early devotional works that combined paint and gold leaf inspired Klimt to an utterly secular exploration of these mixed media. He combines the sinuous movements and sensuous forms of the body with dreamlike stylized arrangements of rhythmic patterns of embossed gold leaf and gold paint.*

THE DEVELOPMENT OF the visual arts during the 20th century has been characterized by an extraordinary diversification of approaches to both the concepts and materials of art. Two of the major protagonists of change were Georges Braque (1882–1963) and Pablo Picasso (1881–1973), who developed the use of collage by incorporating ready-made materials, such as newsprint and wallpaper, into the surface of drawing and painting compositions. The use of collage compounded a fundamental shift in awareness already developed through experiments with Cubist composition, demonstrating that the essence of a painting was in the independent arrangement of the surface shapes and textures rather than in the creation of an illusionistic view. This new development coincided with the political and social upheaval of the First World War, which stimulated a reaction against the established order. In the visual arts this reaction first manifested itself in the absurdist work of the Dada movement and was then further developed by the Surrealists. Artists such as Max Ernst (1891–1976) and Joan Miró (1893–1983) exploited the techniques of mixed media and montage by juxtaposing images in incongruous, disturbing and provocative arrangements that explored the uncon-scious and evoked an interior world of dreams and nightmares.

The dominant figure of this century is Pablo Picasso, who exploited an extraordinary range of materials during his long career. He proved that any material could be

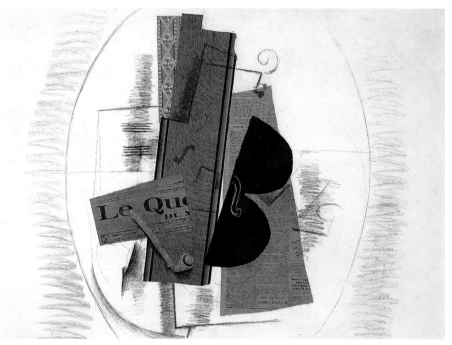

**Georges Braque, *Violin and Pipe*, 1913,**
*29¼ x 39¾ in (75 x 101 cm)*
*Braque first considered the use of ready-made papers as an addition to his still-life drawings in 1912. Braque was the son of a house painter and knew how to create decorative paint effects, such as marbling and false wood grain.*

*He later used this experience by incorporating these techniques along with wallpaper in his paintings. In this composition the combination of collage and charcoal simultaneously emphasizes the picture surface while suggesting space through the overlapping of different media.*

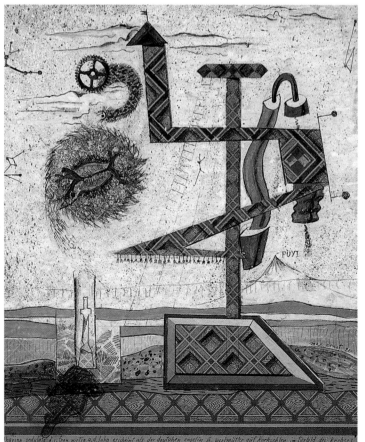

**Max Ernst, *Katarina Ondulata*, 1920,**
*12¼ x 10½ in (31 x 27 cm)*
*Max Ernst's early training was in philosophy, and his work as an artist can be viewed as a visual exploration of the hidden processes of the mind. Individual compositions explore the way the mind filters and retains the memory of experiences by organizing shapes and textures that act as prompts to the imagination. In the lower section of the composition, a strip of wallpaper has been collaged in juxtaposition with painted areas to evoke layers of geological strata. The surface of the upper section contains spattered ink and drawn lines, suggesting distant mountain and clouds.*

**Paul Klee,**
***The Magic Garden,* 1926,**
*19¾ x 16½in (50 x 42 cm)*
*Paul Klee was a master of textural control who experimented with materials and applied a diversity of techniques to create jewel-like surfaces. In his hands, mundane materials transcend their original form, turning into new creative combinations of texture and color that evoke an imaginative reverie. Here he has used a wire mesh mounted on a wooden panel as a support for an application of plaster that has then been inscribed with patterns and stylized images that float in the picture space. The surface has been stained with washes of color that are punctuated by opaque areas of impasto oil paint.*

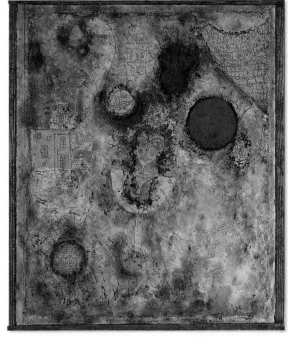

transformed into art by placing familiar materials, such as bicycle saddles in a new context. His treatment of both materials and techniques set a precedent for a level of pictorial invention for all artists in this century. Technological innovations have also provided new printing, photographic, and construction processes as well as new materials, such as acrylics, thus extending the range of pictorial effects available to artists. In the latter half of this century, abstract artists such as Robert Rauschenberg have exploited mass media processes and combined photography and found materials within their artworks.

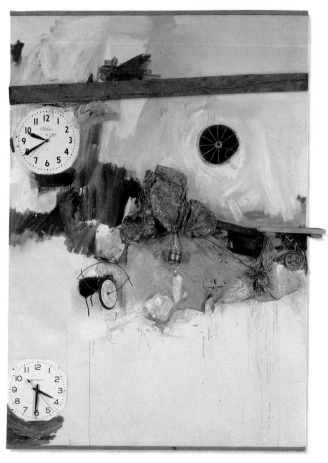

**Robert Rauschenberg,** *Reservoir,* **1961,**
*85½ x 62½ in (234 x 157 cm)*
*Rauschenberg, along with other artists who were affiliated with the Pop Art movement, chose to utilize mass media imagery in combination with found objects and traditional painting media. The relationship between the choice of found objects and the imagery does not work in the manner of a meaningful narrative but as an irrational montage held together as an abstract arrangement through the compositional skills of the artist.*

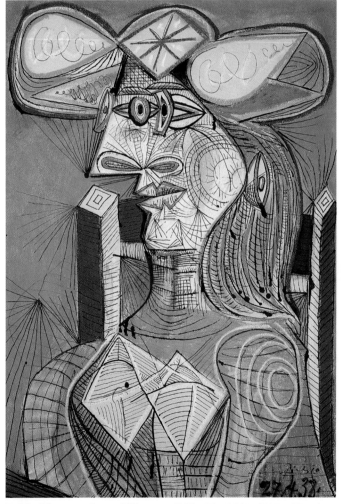

**Pablo Picasso,** *Seated Woman,* **1938,** *30 x 21½ in (76.5 x 55 cm)*
*This composition has been energized by an insistent rhythmic line in pen and ink that gives the forms volume and creates contrasting areas of patterning across the surface of the work. Pastel has been used to create large areas of color that add luminosity to the figure.*

# COMPATIBLE SUPPORTS

THE SURFACE YOU CHOOSE to work on is called a support, and its texture, color, and absorbency will influence the techniques you use to develop a mixed media composition. There is a huge variety of supports for you to explore in combination with mixed media. Try a selection of ready-made supports first and note the different ways your chosen media interact with each one. You can then experiment and create your own supports through a simple process of "priming" and adding a variety of textures and colors to the different surfaces.

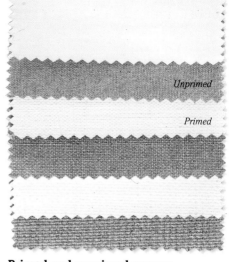

**Primed and unprimed canvas**
*There are two types of canvas available in various weights and widths: artist's linen, made from flax, and cotton duck. You can purchase preprimed canvases or prepare your own.*

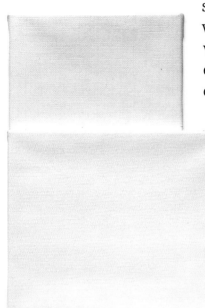

**Commercially prepared boards**
*"Art boards," which have been prepared with either a surface of artists' quality paper or fine textured linen canvas, are suitable for both wet and dry techniques using media such as watercolor and pastel. Precolored art board has a stiff surface and does not buckle when wet. Oil board is primed as a surface for oil and acrylic paint.*

## Choosing the right support

There are a few simple rules to follow to guarantee the life of a mixed media work. Dry drawing media such as charcoal, chalks, and pastels need a support with sufficient tooth to hold the particles of pigment in the surface. Paper, cardboard, and linen supports have a distinct tooth which is ideal for dry media. For this reason, shiny and very smooth surfaces, such as hot pressed paper, are less suitable for extensive working in dry media.

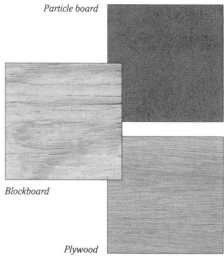

**Suitable wood**
*The most common wood supports for mixed media works are particle board, plywood and blockboard (a type of plywood). These are made from compressed wood dust or layers of wood bonded by glue. Wood panels are the most suitable for building bas-relief surfaces.*

**Suitable paper grounds**
*There is now a huge variety of papers available that are suitable for mixed media compositions. These range from artists' quality paper to handmade colored papers and cardboard. The artists' quality papers are more expensive, but, they can sustain prolonged applications and have a guaranteed longevity.*
*These papers are available in various thicknesses, weights, and textures and are made from 100 percent cotton rag, which does not become brittle and yellow with age. The three standard grades of surface for watercolor papers are Hot-pressed (smooth), NOT (Cold-pressed, semirough), and Rough.*

**Water and oil-based media**

The main criteria to bear in mind when choosing supports is whether they are suitable for wet or dry media. Water-based media require a support of sufficient absorbency to hold the liquid but not so absorbent that the color sinks and loses its brilliance. For this reason manufacturers add size to paper to reduce its absorbency. Water-based media will cause a support to buckle as the surface absorbs the water, so the thicker the paper you choose the less dramatic the buckling will be and the more capable it will be of weathering heavy treatment.

When working with oil-based media, it is generally recommended that you prepare the surface of your support with an acrylic primer because the oil will damage the surface of unprimed paper, board, or canvas. Priming also reduces the absorbency of the support and stops acrylics and oil-based media from sinking into the surface and losing brilliance. A colored support will interact with overlaid pigments and when combined with a textured surface the result will be attractive broken color effect on the surface of the paper or canvas.

**Handmade and manufactured papers**
*There is a vast range of colored and textured papers for you to use available from art and paper stores in single sheets, pads, and rolls. An increasingly diverse selection of papers are now being made which incorporate various plant fibers such as flax, onion skin, and bracken. These papers make highly attractive and surprising supports for mixed media work and are used to create a dominant texture in a collage or print work.*

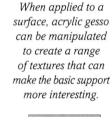

*Primer with PVA glue and sand*

*Basic primer*

*Thickly primed board*

**Gesso**
*When applied to a surface, acrylic gesso can be manipulated to create a range of textures that can make the basic support more interesting.*

**Primed Boards**
*To create a luminous background, boards need to be primed with a suitable primer, such as acrylic primer or gesso, before paint is applied. Boards can also be primed with colored gessos made by adding acrylic paint, or they can be primed with PVA and sand to create texture.*

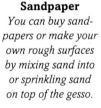

**Sandpaper**
*You can buy sandpapers or make your own rough surfaces by mixing sand into or sprinkling sand on top of the gesso.*

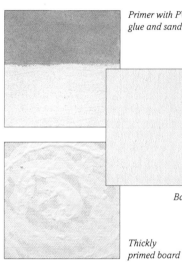

**Using gesso with additives**
*Various materials can be added to gesso to create an exciting textured or colored surface in bas-relief. Sand, string, dried grasses, and grains will all create interesting surfaces. You can also add sawdust, stone dust, or any other inert powdered material to PVA glue, acrylic primer, or gesso to create an interesting diversity of textures to work on. By adding a water-based paint or dried pigment, such as charcoal dust or crushed chalk pastel, you can tint the primer to any color. Additional materials can be applied in several ways: you can sprinkle or embed them in the wet surface of the gesso so that the color and tone of the materials remains evident, or you can mix the materials into the gesso so that they all become the same color.*

# DRAWING MATERIALS

A NUMBER OF DRAWING MATERIALS are suitable for mixed media, and they can be used in almost any combination. Since each drawing medium will produce a range of marks of a different density, tone, and texture, it is a good idea to explore the scope of line and tone that each produces before you experiment with them in combination. It is also important to find sympathetic combinations of drawing media that will enhance rather than detract from each other. Drawing media that are alike, such as charcoal and chalks, will work unobtrusively together, whereas media with disimilar qualities such as wax crayons and inks will create dramatic qualities of contrast. This is because the water and the wax resist each other and create distinctive patterns.

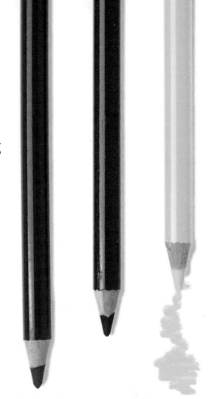

DRAWING MEDIA can be categorized into those that share similar characteristics (watercolor and ink are both wet) and those that use a common method of application (pastel and chalk are both rubbed on the support). Dry media are those that can be applied without a brush for example charcoal, pastels, and crayons. Wet drawing media are those that are either suspended in a liquid medium or require diluting before use.

**Colored charcoal pencils**
*Colored charcoal pencils are the same as pastel crayons, only they are slightly harder and encased in wood. Their chalky constitution makes them more suitable for subtle blending techniques and ideal for very fine detailed work.*

**Felt-tip pens**
*Felt-tip pens are a relatively recent addition to the repertoire of drawing materials. The range of marks they produce is limited but they are popular for techniques requiring a bold line and strong color saturation.*

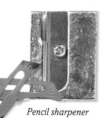

**Sharpening**
*Hard pastels and charcoal can be sharpened using a pencil sharpener or sharp blade to gently pare the end to a point.*

*Pencil sharpener and blades*

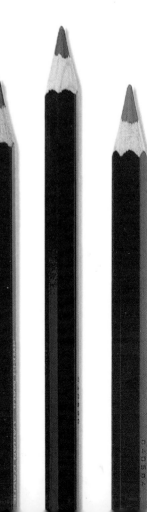

*Graphite pencil*

*Kneaded eraser*

**Kneaded erasers**
*Kneaded erasers are suitable for erasing a range of dry drawing media. They can be pulled and kneaded into a fine point for detailed work. You can effectively use this type of eraser as a drawing tool, creating highlights in a work as you remove the pigment and reveal the surface of the support below.*

**Water-soluble pencils**
*Water-soluble pencils are used in the same manner as other pencils to create a linear drawing and areas of shading. The drawing is then washed over with a wet brush. This transforms the linear marks by dispersing the color to create a wash drawing. Rich color effects can also be achieved by drawing directly on a damp surface to disperse the pigment.*

## Wax crayons
*Wax crayons are popular for resist techniques where a drawing is first developed in wax crayon and then worked over with a wash of watercolor or ink. The wax repels the water-based medium and shows through the layer in striking contrast. Crayons can also be overlaid on top of each other and scratched off to reveal the layers below.*

## Fixatives
The surface of a mixed media work that incorporates dry media like charcoal and pastel is easily spoiled by smudging. You can avoid this by giving the work a light spray of fixative to fix the particles of pigment to the paper. Fixative is also used to build up a work in layers of different dry pigments by spraying and fixing each successive layer of color. The fixative will alter the work by slightly darkening some of the tones. With pastel work it is very important not to overspray since this will destroy the inherent "bloom" of the pastels. For this reason some artists do not fix the last layer, or else choose to spray only the back of their work.

## Willow charcoal and charcoal pencil
*Charcoal is carbonated wood that comes in various thicknesses. Paper which will readily accept charcoal is easy to erase and alter. Charcoal can be pared and filed to a point with a blade or by rubbing its edge on glass paper. Charcoal also comes compressed in stick and pencil form that produces a dense, velvet black.*

*Types of charcoal*

*Reed pen*

*Technical pen*

## Pen and ink
*There is a variety of inks available, the main types being the water- and shellac-based inks. Shellac-based inks are waterproof when dry and are suitable for techniques of overpainting when you do not want the ink line to spread and bleed into subsequent washes of color. Inks also come in a full range of colors from black to the full spectrum of luminous primaries and secondaries. Inks can be worked with different tools including nib pens, reed pens, and sable, bristle, or synthetic brushes. A particular advantage of inks is their ability to be worked in dilutions of water, making it possible to produce monochrome works in a subtle gradation of tones.*

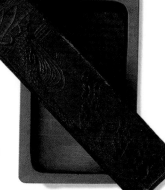

*Chinese inks are sold in either sticks or bottles. The ink can then be diluted with water in a small stone well. The art of using a Chinese brush is to hold the brush vertically or diagonally so that you can vary the thickness of the line from a delicate trace, using the tip, to a full broad stroke, using the heel of the brush.*

*Chinese block ink*

*Basic pen and ink*

*Chinese brushes*

*Soft pastels*

## Soft pastels and Conté crayons
*Soft pastels are essentially pure pigment held lightly in a gum solution. The soft-grained texture produced is ideal for painting because of its ease of application and blending qualities. Conté crayons are basically harder pastels with a denser texture and they are ideal for detailed work. Both types of pastel are available in a huge range of colors.*

*Colored Conté crayons*

# PAINTING MATERIALS

EVERY PAINTING MEDIUM has particular qualities of texture and color, and all are suitable for mixed media techniques. Painting media can be broadly classified as water-based and oil-based. Water-based media include watercolors, gouache, tempera, poster colors, and acrylics. Oil-based colors include oil paint, oil bars, pastels, and wax encaustic, which is thinned using turpentine or mineral spirits. Media that share similar qualities, such as watercolor and gouache, are readily used in any combination. Mixing oil- and water-based paints requires more careful consideration.

**Oil bars**
*Oil bars are applied in the manner of an oil pastel, by rubbing the medium into the support. They can be further diluted on the support using a brush and turpentine.*

*Crushed chalk pastels*

*Fine hog hair oil brush (No. 10)*

*Fine hog hair oil brush (No. 12)*

**Brushes and palettes**
*Oil paint can be mixed on either a hand-held palette or on a smooth impermeable sheet of board or glass. There is a specialist palette for acrylics – a tray that keeps the paints moist to prolong mixing time. Both oils and acrylic paints can be used with a range of brushes.*

ALL PAINTS ARE MADE from colored pigments suspended in a medium. This allows the pigment to be controlled in a fluid state and to dry to form a durable surface. Each type of paint has a distinct quality of handling and will have an advantage over other painting media for certain techniques. The advantage of water-based paints is that they generally dry quickly, allowing for speed of application and ease of alteration. The acacia gum used in watercolor and gouache paints allows you to over-paint in layers without picking up the dried underlying color. The gum also allows you to make alterations by simply wetting and lifting the color from the support

using a sponge or tissue. Acrylic paints are also water soluble but, unlike watercolor, they dry to an insoluble plastic film. Acrylics can be used in transparent washes, but they are also suitable for using in impasto to add texture. Manufacturers have developed a range of additives, which you can add to alter the paint or retard the drying time to allow for more

**Palette knives and scrapers**
*Palette knives are used for mixing paint on a palette. Painting knives are similar, but they are specifically shaped and angled to apply the paint to the support. Scrapers are used to drag and scrape paint across the surface of a wide support and to create linear patterns.*

*Alizarin Crimson (oil)*

*Cadmium Yellow (oil)*

*Phthalo Blue (oil)*

*Phthalo Green (acrylic)*

*Titanium White (acrylic)*

*Ultramarine Blue (acrylic)*

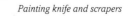
*Painting knife and scrapers*

controlled blending of colors. All water-based media are suitable for overlayering in different drawing and oil-based media.

## Oil paints

Oil paint is a popular medium because of its ease of manipulation. Combined with its scope of color and texture, it generally surpasses water-based media. Oil paint dries slowly and is most commonly used in the "a la prima" technique of painting wet-in-wet. When used in a wash (or impasto), oil paint is suitable for receiving oil pastels and oil bars, but it will repel water-based media. It is very important to use artists'-quality paints where possible, since the pigments used in the paints have been tested and are known to be of a highly durable nature.

*Watercolor brushes: mixed sable Nos. 12 and 8*

*Gamboge*

*Windsor Green*

*Tortillons*

*Scarlet Lake*

## Resist technique

*The simplest way to create a resist technique is to apply an application of an oil-based medium such as wax crayon, grease pencils, or oil pastel to a composition. These media repel water and show through the subsequent watercolor wash. Another excellent resist medium is masking fluid, which can be used to create subtle color variations.*

*Masking fluid*

## Watercolor

*Watercolors are made of pigment suspended in gum solution and have different degrees of lightfastness, depending on the type of pigment. Watercolors can be built up in layers of transparent washes. They can also be lifted from the support by wetting and wiping away with a sponge.*

*Cerulean Blue*

## Sponge rollers

*Rollers are useful for applying liquid paint to a support. You can use small foam rollers, which are suitable for watercolor, or decorators' rollers for larger works in acrylics and oils. Rollers can either amplify or unify the texture of a support.*

## Sponges and tortillons

*Sponges are used for lifting water from the surface, but they can also be used to apply paint. Tortillons can be used to blend details in pastel works.*

*Natural sponge*

*Coarse sponge*

## Oil pastels

*Oil pastel is bound by oil, providing a rich depth of tone and a distinct degree of transparency. Oil pastels are not readily displaced and, as a consequence, do not require the use of fixative. They can be used in impasto and, when diluted with spirits, moved around on the support as a wash of color.*

*Roller*

# CHARCOAL AND BLACK INK

CHARCOAL AND BLACK INK are two tonal drawing media whose contrasting qualities of wet and dry create exciting mixed media combinations. The dry nature of charcoal produces a delightful range of tones and marks – from faint delicate traces and scumbled broken applications to a rich velvet black. The density of ink can be altered by adding water and can be applied with a range of tools from sable and Chinese brushes, to reed and metal-nib pens. Using these two media together, you will have the freedom to exploit drawing to its optimum tonal range.

## Texture and pattern

This drawing demonstrates the contrasting qualities of charcoal and ink and the expressive range of marks that both media can produce. There is a contrived tension in the composition achieved by the close arrangement of the foreground figures and the dramatic shift in scale of figures in the background. The artist has used various techniques to emphasize the textures and features of the women's clothing. In contrast to the subtle areas of tone created by the charcoal, the artist has blocked in the dense area of black using a brush and ink in the jumper of the figure on the right.

## Ink and charcoal

*Ink and charcoal react in contrasting ways with the paper support. Whereas the charcoal is effectively filed away by the tooth of the paper, creating a grainy texture, the ink soaks into the surface of the paper. This absorption produces a wet effect known as bleeding, where the ink is dispersed across the paper surface.*

## Frottage

*Frottage is the technique of using the side or blunt end of a stick of charcoal, crayon, or graphite to take a rubbing off a textured surface. This shows the texture of the wooden grain of a drawing board, but you can also take rubbings from stone and artificial materials.*

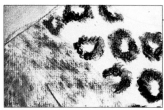

**By drawing charcoal** across the paper around the woman's collar, the artist has utilized the grain of the paper to amplify the texture of the support, giving the clothing a realistic appearance.

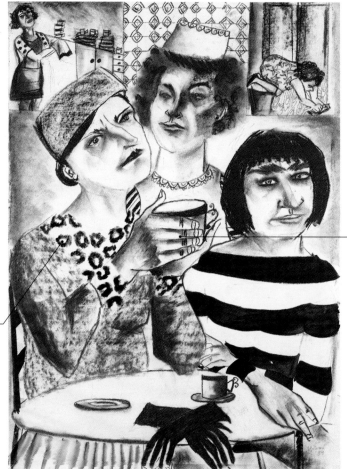

**Hilary Rosen, *Cafe*, 1989, charcoal and ink**

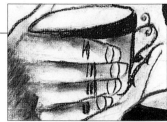

**The hand and cup** have a clearly defined contour with the fingers, created by variations in light and shade and outlined in ink. The artist has blended the charcoal into the paper with her fingers, creating areas of depth and lighter touches.

## Contrasting effects

The abstract image below also concentrates on the creative possibilities of line and tone. Two contrasting qualities of tone are created by using similar media with diffferent methods of application. The ink is applied with a brush to contrast with areas of tone created by the use of spray paint. The recurrent use of cellular shapes evokes a feeling of organic growth rather than describing any specific plant form.

The artist has created an ambiguously witty play of lines and patterns that draws the viewer into translating this abstract arrangement. In the construction of this imaginative work, the flow of the rhythmical marks is uninterrupted by any hesitation or correction, creating an air of confident improvisation. Looking carefully into the compostion you can see the way the artist has developed complex relationships between the shapes. Some are enclosed cells, others are open, some contain nuclei and others appear to be gyrating, bending, or splitting. Each delineated shape has its own unique character while maintaining a general resemblance to the other shapes.

### CHINESE INK

Chinese ink is a very expressive medium which requires disciplined control. The great Chinese masters of this medium would first study their subject for long periods of time until they understood its form. Working on a roll of rice paper, they would lay on diluted washes and marks in undiluted black. The art of controlling a Chinese brush is to vary the angle of the brush to the support, holding the brush vertically using the tip and at an angle using the heel of the brush. By pressing and lifting the brush you can vary the line from thin traces to broad expressive sweeps.

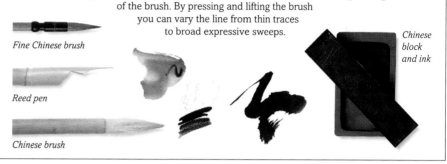

*Fine Chinese brush*

*Reed pen*

*Chinese brush*

*Chinese block and ink*

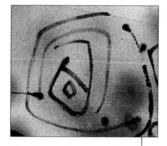

**The linen** texture of the support creates a broken line as the ink is drawn across the absorbent surface.

**Marks retain** the echo of the action that created them and in this example the quality of the line reflects an angular wrist action. This is in direct contrast with the diffuse and erratic character of the spray paint.

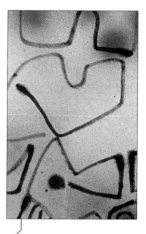

### USING A DIFFUSER

A mouth diffuser is used by holding the two tubes at right angles to each other and immersing the end of the longer tube in the paint. Holding the shorter end, with the plastic mouthpiece between your lips, blow firmly; your breath will draw the fluid up the longer tube and atomize the liquid into a fine spray. You can vary the spray you produce by altering the pressure of your breath and the distance and angle at which you hold the diffuser from the support.

Hold the spray in a single stationary position to create a starlike explosion of ink, or sweep the diffuser across the page to give a wider and finer coverage.

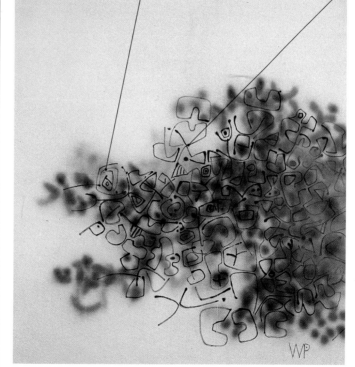

**Wendy Pasmore, RA,** *Untitled,* **1991, spray paint and ink**

**Visual invention**
In contrast with the complexity of the shapes, defined by the ink lines, a unifying tone has been created using spray paint. The beauty of this work lies in the clarity and simplicity of its construction, which echoes the principles of Chinese painting. Artworks such as this simply evoke the energy of nature in just the same way that the rhythm and structure of music evoke the natural harmonies and movements of the elements.

# CHARCOAL AND PASTELS

CHARCOAL IS A HIGHLY VERSATILE drawing medium. Its inert nature makes it highly suitable for laying down a drawing design before over-painting in a water- or oil-based medium. As a tonal drawing medium, charcoal is commonly overworked with additional dry coloring media such as chalks and pastels. Esthetically, charcoal and pastel work well together, and by using the two media, you can achieve subtle traces of line, delicate transitions of blended tone, and dense applications of bold marks. A considerable advantage of these media is that they are easily erased and manipulated, which allows for great freedom of compositional movement. Because of this, it is necessary to preserve your work carefully by fixing the surface with a light spray of fixative (see p.15).

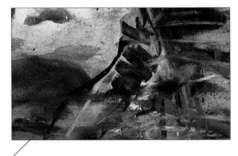

**Pastel and charcoal**
*The responsive nature of these media encourages a sensitivity of touch and subtlety of manipulation. You can work pastel and charcoal either as lines or as areas of tone by altering their angle to the support and by working with either the edge or the side of the media.*

**Pigments**
*Both charcoal and pastel are capable of an exciting array of marks, depending on the action of the hand and how much pressure is applied. With all dry drawing media it is the raised tooth of the support that files away the particles of pigment, so the harder you press, the more pigment is deposited on the surface.*

**A very open** pattern of marks created in a limited color range has been used to define the rocks and sky. The artist has blocked in areas with black ink and charcoal and then covered the area in pastel, to suggest the rock strata.

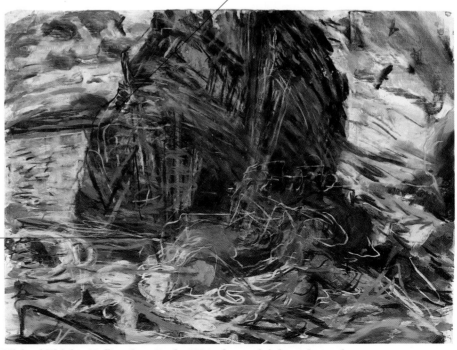

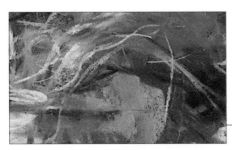

**To emphasize** the dramatic movement of the waves and wind against the weathered form of the rock, the artist has overlaid linear traces of white and ochre pastel onto blended sweeps of pink and gray. These colorful patterns give the whole piece a sense of movement.

**Michael Wright, *Mullion Cove Rocks*, 1994, charcoal, ink, and pastel**

## Female head

In this image, in contrast with the previous painting, the charcoal has been very subtly blended with the pastel to create a blurred effect. The simplified form and full frontal angle of vision produce an eerie stillness. Paradoxically, the apparent symmetry of the composition amplifies all the nuances of asymmetry contained within the features of the face. This means that our attention is focused on the slight shifts and movements in the form of the features. This is an emotionally taut image, full of a subtle pathos that is expressed in the physical working of the surface. Nervous touches of pastel which have been swept across the woman's features, simultaneously emphasize her emotional intensity and blur the details of her features.

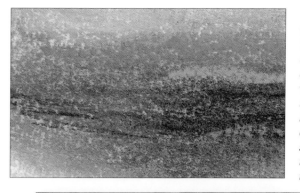

### Creating details

*To produce facial details in charcoal and pastel, you should aim to combine the two mediums with confident subtlety. To create these lips, a rich vermilion pastel has been streaked across a line of charcoal. In the image below the smudged lipstick effect amplifies the masklike appearance of the woman.*

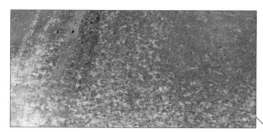

**A technique of** subtle blending has been used in this detail of the neck. Pastel has been worked into the surface of the support with a finger in order to merge the pastel powder with the previous application of charcoal.

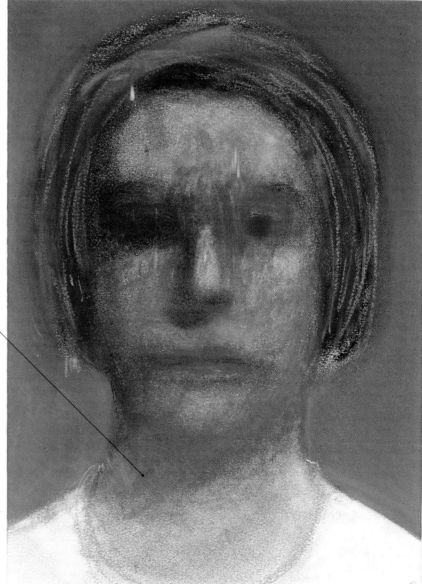

## Soft pastels

*Used in their full strength, colored pastels are an extremely powerful coloring medium. However, immensely subtle modeling can be achieved by using the wide range of subtle tints that are available in each of the colors.*

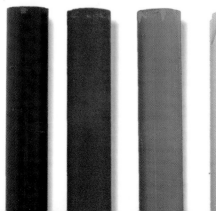

**Robert Clatworthy, *Female head II*, 1993, charcoal and pastel**

### Pastel dust

*Soft pastels are pure pigment, bound in a light solution of gum with the addition of chalk to create subtle tints. Pastel can easily be reduced to dust by paring it with a knife. The dust can then be applied to a composition using a brush or cotton ball to create a dry wash of color.*

# LINE AND COLOR

THE MOST COMMON TECHNIQUE for combining line and color is to add a watercolor wash to a linear drawing medium. The outline is established in graphite, charcoal, or ink to create a strong linear arrangement. Once you are satisfied with the organization of line, you can apply washes of watercolor in increasing strength to add body to the linear structure.

### Combining colors

In this expressive rendition of a familiar subject, the artist has created strong linear movements and patterns in charcoal to contrast with vibrant washes of watercolor. The weight of the sunflower heads and compact foliage have been amplified by the application of dense line and saturated color. The work has been completed using a delicate linear drawing in chalk to define the texture of the curling leaves. The artist has successfully combined an analysis of the plant itself with an experiment in mark-making.

### Surface interaction

*Wet media in the form of watercolor will interact with the surface texture of the support very differently from an application of a dry medium such as charcoal or chalk. The watercolor will retain the shape of the brushstroke and will settle into the pitted hollows of the surface in tiny pools of pigment – a dry medium will catch in the raised surface.*

**The benefit of** using charcoal as a drawing media is that it can be easily manipulated, allowing for alterations before adding a watercolor wash. Charcoal has been used here to create a linear pattern over a watercolor wash that points up the texture and form of the sunflower.

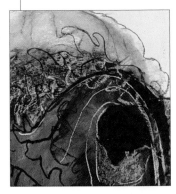

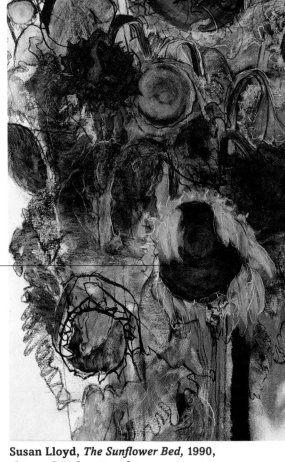

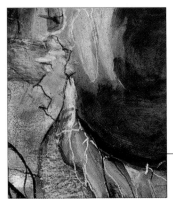

**Wet and dry media** used in combination create areas of textural contrast. Here the saturated areas of color, created by watercolor, contrast with the dry texture of the white pastel which has been overlaid in broken lines. The areas of charcoal have been created to give the piece a strong linear structure and added definition.

**Susan Lloyd, *The Sunflower Bed*, 1990, charcoal and watercolor**

### Ink and wash

*Watercolor and inks can be used in different combinations to create effects of either a clear line or bleeding. Here a sepia line was drawn across a watercolor wash while the wash was still wet.*

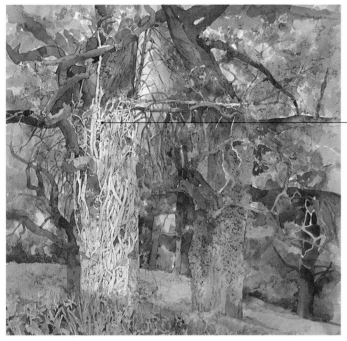

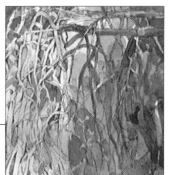

**The artist has** created a complex linear structure in sepia ink to define the ivy which has then been overlaid with delicate tints of neutral washes. A single area has been left free of color to focus the viewer's attention on the detailed drawing of the ivy.

**Valerie Claypole,** *Ivy Entwined Oaks,* **1988, watercolor and ink**

## Controlled color

This is a subtle and complex work in which the artist has painstakingly observed the growth of ivy as it envelops the gnarled forms of the oak trees. The linear composition has been developed first in pencil and then in clear unbroken line using pen and sepia ink. Delicately controlled washes have been carefully applied to add color to the composition. The artist has strived to establish a balance between line and color throughout the composition without obscuring the linear work. The color key to this composition is a harmony of greens that serves to highlight the parasitic colorless form of the ivy embracing the central tree.

## Using color as shape

Bob Baggaley's semiabstract work is based on memories of traveling through the Cumbrian landscape. The linear drawing was established using a fountain pen. It was subsequently overworked in saturated washes of watercolor. The striking arrangement of washes evokes the drama of a moonlit night. The light areas of the composition are amplified by the deep blue of the surrounding border that frames the scene in the manner of a window. Baggaley trained during the sixties and assimilated the Pop Art and abstract influences of this period into a later preoccupation with landscape imagery. These influences can be seen in the deliberate play of positive and negative shape, in the use of the white of the paper, and in the artist's evident delight in the abstract emphasis of the paint surface.

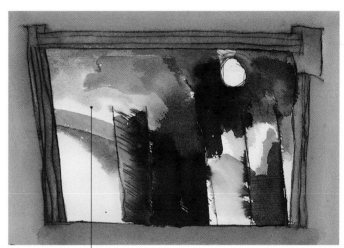

**Bob Baggaley,** *Westward,* **1989, watercolor and ink**

**The washes of color** have been loosely applied wet-into-wet, allowing the colors to run and create secondary mixtures of color. The overworking of watercolor on ink has caused the ink to lift and bleed into the colors of the washes.

### WATERCOLOR TECHNIQUES

Watercolor is an ideal medium to use in combination with drawing media, to either add tone in a monochrome wash or add color in the full range of hues and tints. Depending on the texture of the support and the technique of application, it is possible to achieve a wide range of expressive qualities of wash. You can create dramatically different effects by working wet-over-dry or wet-into-wet, or by combinations of these two techniques.

 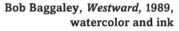 

*Wash on dry wash*
*By laying a wash, allowing it to dry, and applying subsequent washes in confident single applications, you can achieve the effect of distinct overlapping layers of color. Where the layers overlap, the colors will mix optically to create a secondary color.*

*Bleeding wet-into-wet*
*By applying a wash of color to a wet area of the support or to a previous wash in a wet state, you can explore dramatic and spontaneous color effects. The colors will run and merge into each other, creating new colors and feathering movements in the paint.*

*Scumbling*
*Use the side of a semidry brush to drag a light trace of pigment across the raised tooth of artist's textured watercolor paper. The effect created is one of a broken surface of color that allows the previous wash or tone of the support to show through in sparkling flecks of light.*

# RESIST TECHNIQUES

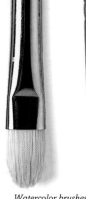

*Oil pastels*

*Watercolor brushes*

ONE INTERESTING MIXED MEDIA EFFECT is created using resist techniques, which capitalize on the tendency of oil to repel water. There is a wide range of oil-based media suitable for resist techniques, including oil paint, oil pastels, and wax crayons. Another useful resist medium is masking fluid. A design is created using the fluid and overpainting in a wash of watercolor or ink. The resist medium adheres to the support and shows through the subsequent wash of water-based media. Experimenting with resist techniques allows you to exploit bold contrasts of color or to work with a more subtle range of contrasts with a closer range of tones. You can use an opaque oil-based color to contrast with a subsequent wash, or you can apply a transparent oil or wax medium that will allow the tone of the support or prior layer of color to show through.

## Using wax resist

The master British sculptor Henry Moore consistently used resist techniques in his drawings. In this small sketchbook composition he has pursued a sculptural theme of interior and exterior form by using transparent white and yellow wax crayons to portray a wire armature sculptors use as a support for plaster or clay. This technique defines the inner structure of the head. The abstract network of wax lines glows through the subsequent wash of dark gray watercolor. The final details of human features have been achieved with a cursive stroke of black chalk on the contour of the head, and brushstrokes of black India ink to define the nose, mouth, and eyes.

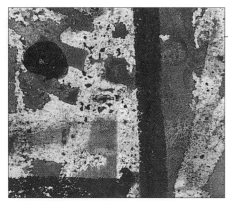

**It is possible** to clearly see the way in which the wax repels and causes the watercolor to collect in little spots on the surface of the wax crayon. The density of the shellac-based India-ink drawing has allowed the black line to partially cover the wax crayon in a broken line and magnifies the resist effect on the surface.

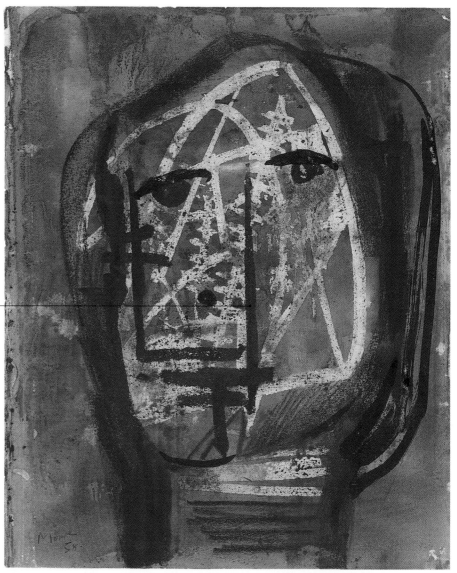

**Henry Moore, *Female head,* 1958, wax crayon, watercolor and ink**

## Lifting and patterning

The artist chose "Mirage" as the title of this work because the quality of the light and color suggests the presence of a landscape suffused in a shimmering heat. The work has been developed using an original approach to watercolor.

The bands of watercolor that wash across the upper section of the painting have been patterned using plastic bubble wrap. The bubble wrap has partly displaced and partly lifted the watercolor from the surface of the support, leaving a distinct pattern. This process was repeated using crumpled foil to overlay the middle section, creating a complex overlayering of the two patterns.

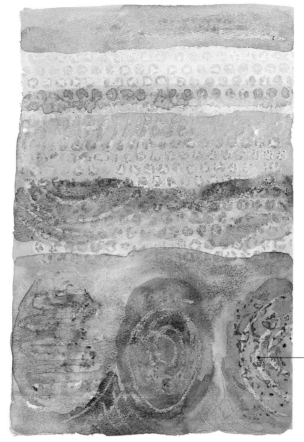

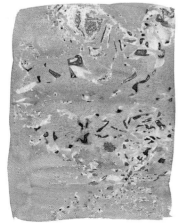

**Masking fluid**
*This is a latex liquid which is applied with a brush or dip pen to mask out areas of an artwork. After a subsequent wash has dried, the masking fluid can be gently rubbed away to reveal the underlying color.*

**Kate Nicholson, *Mirage*, 1994, wax crayon and watercolor**

**Washes of saturated** colors have been bled into each other over concentric circles of pink wax resist line. Before the watercolor dried, the artist pressed a crumpled sheet of aluminum foil into the surface using a book as a weight to displace some of the color.

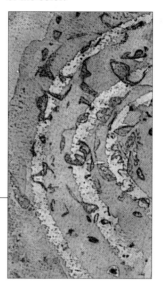

---

### TECHNIQUES FOR LIFTING AND PATTERNING WATERCOLOR

An exciting variety of textures can be created within the surface of water-based media by pressing materials into the wet paint. Choose nonabsorbent materials that have either a distinct texture such as bubble wrap, or materials that can be folded and crumpled to create a texture, such as foil or grease-proof paper.

You can also experiment using thin wire, string, and grasses. Place the material onto a wash of color while it is still wet and then apply pressure using a book or board. Lift the material away from the painting as the paint is close to drying and a distinct pattern will remain.

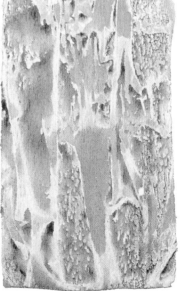

**Bubble plastic**
*The bubble wrap has been applied in the same manner as the foil, left. The uniform orange wash has been drawn in a cellular pattern that has effectively taken a print of the surface of the bubbles in the wrap.*

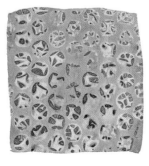

**Creased aluminum foil**
*In this watercolor wash you can see the patterning created by the use of the foil. The foil has displaced the watercolor into pools of deep color and the result is similar to light playing on water.*

**Plastic wrap**
*Placed in contact with the watercolor, the surface of the plastic wrap has created a complex pattern akin to marbling.*

**Materials**

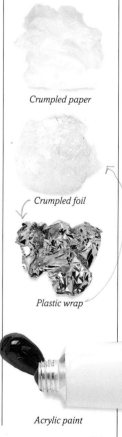

*Crumpled paper*

*Crumpled foil*

*Plastic wrap*

*Acrylic paint*

# GALLERY OF DRAWING

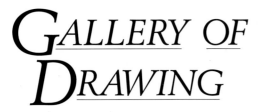

D RAWING IS THE MOST fundamental language of visual expression and employs the simplest of media in the forms of graphite, charcoal, ink, and chalk. The directness of application when using drawing media allows the artist to develop a composition rapidly in line and tone and to focus on the primary task of organizing a meaningful design. There are many examples of drawings in which artists have enhanced their work using either watercolor, chalks, or pastel.

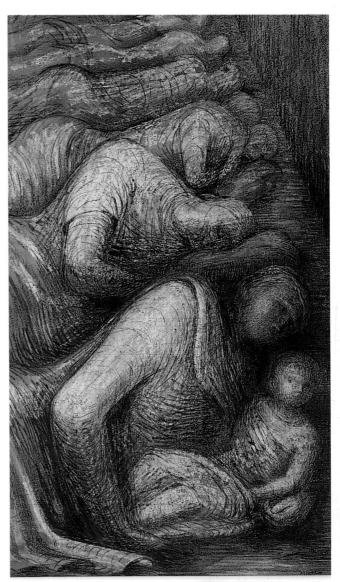

**Henry Moore, *Row of Sleepers*, 1941, pen, ink, chalk, crayon, and watercolor** *21½ x 12½ in (54.5 x 32 cm)*
*Henry Moore (1898–1986) is best known for his international work as a sculptor and his monumental treatment of form was profoundly influenced by pre-Columbian and Romanesque carving. He was commissioned as a war artist during the Second World War and made a series of moving studies of people taking refuge in the London subway. This composition, which has religious associations with the Madonna and Child, was developed using his unique technique of overlaying wax lines and ink with watercolor.*

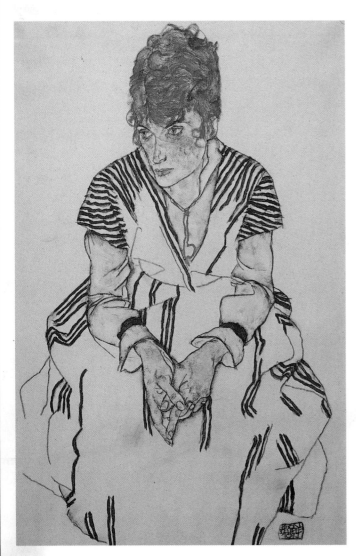

**Egon Schiele, *Adele Harms Seated in a Striped Dress*, 1917, gouache, watercolor, and pencil on paper** *7 x 4½ in (17.5 x 11 cm)*
*Egon Schiele's (1890–1918) distinctive style was influenced by and partly developed as a reaction to the rhythmical patterns and decorative use of color in the Art Nouveau movement. In this beautifully observed study Schiele's economical control of line, using graphite, is complimented by a limited palette of warm and cool colors applied in a scumbled application of gouache adding volume to the figures.*

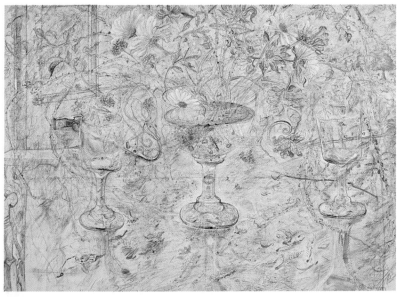

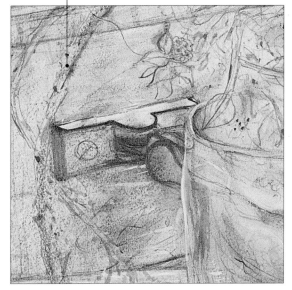

**David Jones,** *Flora in Calix Light,* **1950,**
**pencil and watercolor** *22¼ x 30¼ in (56.5 x 76.5 cm)*
*David Jones (1895–1974) was both an artist and a poet. In this luminous reverie on light playing through delicate forms of flowers and glass bowls, he creates a flux of rhythmic movements that lead the eye on a spiraling journey through the composition. The substance of matter is tranformed and replaced by transparent veils of light and shadow created through the delicate use of line and nervous touches of watercolor.*

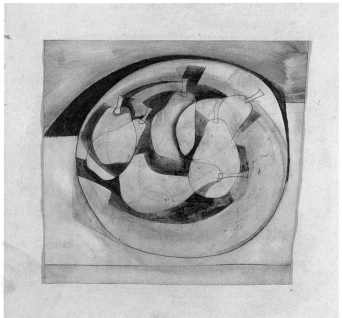

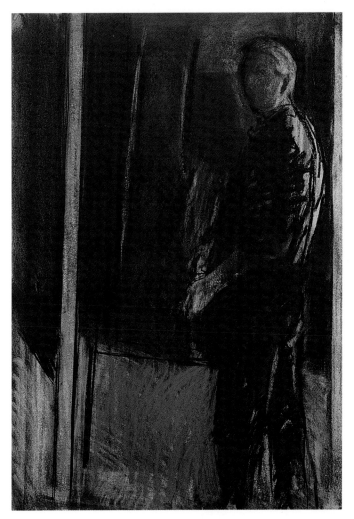

**Ben Nicholson,** *Plate of Pears,* **1955,**
**pencil and oil wash on paper** *12 x 13⅜ in (30.5 x 33 cm)*
*The drawing's flat surface is emphasized by hatching (closely spaced parallel lines) on the stained surface. An illusion of form is created by overlapping the shapes to create silhouettes.*

**Peter Coker RA,** *Le Peintre au Travail,*
**1994, mixed media** *31 x 22 in (76 x 56 cm)*
*In this drawing, Coker uses chalk and pastel in a limited palette of black and somber earth colors, creating a tension between the presence of the figure and the surrounding structure of the room.*

# MULTILAYERED COMPOSITIONS

WATER-BASED MEDIA can be used in combination with a range of other paints to create works of multiple layers. One of the best media to use for multilayered compositions is acrylic. This is because the rapid drying time of acrylic paint allows overworking without disturbing the previous application of color. Watercolor and gouache can be transformed into paints with acrylic qualities by adding PVA (polyvinyl acetate) to the pigment. You can also paint layers of PVA over water-based washes to effectively seal the paint and allow a subtle build up of colored layers.

## Using PVA glue

This artist has developed a technique of building up an image in layers of gouache and PVA, adding passages of ink to define the strata and texture of the forms in the landscape. By mixing PVA with the gouache or applying it in a wash, the PVA soaks into the pigment, giving the chalky gouache a depth and richness of color. PVA in a liquid state is opaque white, but it dries into a transparent plastic film, sealing the absorbent gouache and stopping the ink from sinking into the surface. The effect of combining the black ink and gouache washes is akin to the contrast created by the leadwork surrounding luminous areas of stained glass.

Craig Peacock's paintings are lyrical interpretations of landscape and his work is in the tradition of the British Neoromantics, echoing the work of artists such as Graham Sutherland in his concern with the way the imagination transforms the memory of landscape.

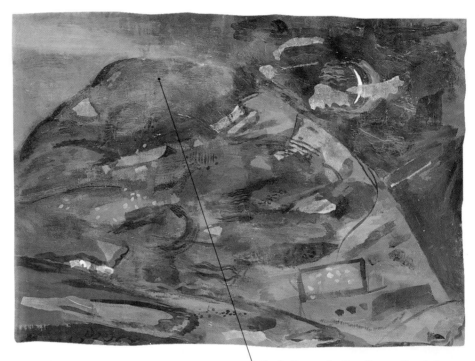

**Craig Peacock, *Landscape Cumbria*, 1993, acrylic and gouache**

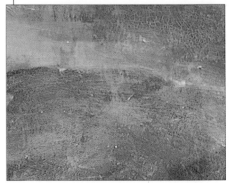

**In this part of the** composition the artist has overlaid a thin pale wash of gouache and PVA to push back the underlying black ink lines. This has created a quality of mist in contrast with the more strident tones lower down in the composition.

## WET-ON-DRY TECHNIQUE

A richly varied and textured quality of color can be created in a painting by working layers of color over each other, using the different qualities of both wet and dry mixed media. You can create the effects of layers of transparent, semitransparent, and opaque color by overlaying acrylics and gouache and using a technique of wet-on-dry.

**Suspension**
*The black ink line is suspended between two semitransparent layers of color by a wash of diluted PVA applied between each wash of pigment.*

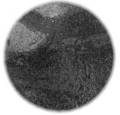

**Optical mixing**
*A wash of vermilion acrylic has had an application of saturated red and magenta gouache dragged across it to create the broken effect of optical mixture.*

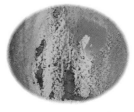

**Complementary colors**
*Turquoise and ochre oil pastels have resisted a wash of orange acrylic and magenta gouache to create a surface of flecks of complementary colors.*

## Building up the layers

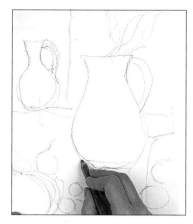

1 ◀ Begin by grouping a small collection of objects, such as pitchers, fruit, and leaves, then set the arrangement against tissue paper of a complementary color. Looking carefully at your still life, roughly sketch in the outlines of the various objects with a soft, pastel pencil on a sheet of handmade watercolor paper.

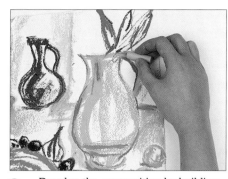

2 ▲ Develop the composition by building up the image with a variety of oil pastels to create areas of vivid and intense color.

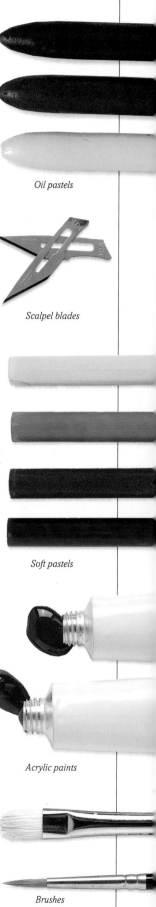

*Oil pastels*

*Scalpel blades*

*Soft pastels*

*Acrylic paints*

*Brushes*

3 ▶ Using a wash brush for the larger areas, and a fine brush for the details, paint over the oil pastel with washes of acrylic. To add more depth you can vary the thickness of the application of acrylic paint. Here a bright pink has been used on the pitcher.

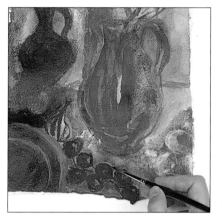

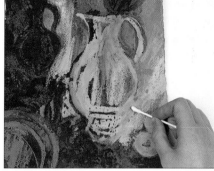

4 ▲ Make subtle alterations to the surface by overworking with a cotton ball to remove pastel, adding texture and detail.

### Still life

Lucinda Cobley trained as an illustrator and her work, like much contemporary illustration, crosses the boundaries between design and fine art. She uses a variety of mixed media techniques, and here she has chosen to work on handmade paper and use the torn edge to interact with the forms in the composition. The surface treatment and the rough edging encourages us to view the work as a surface of beauty rather than a simple view of objects. To fully exploit the contrasting textures and colors of the different media, an open treatment of mark-making is used in preference to detailed observations.

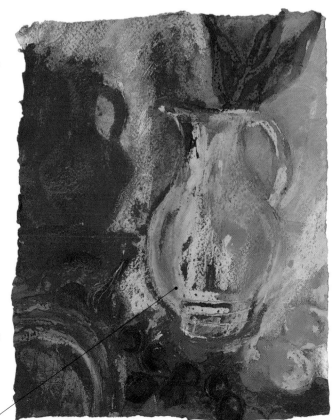

**A rich turquoise** oil pastel has been overlaid by saturated washes of violet gouache and vermilion acrylic paint. The overall effect is one of a rich layering by working colors over each other using various broken-color techniques. One of the most effective of these methods is scumbling, which involves dragging dry paint across the raised tooth of the support.

# OIL AND SOFT PASTELS

PASTELS ARE MADE from pure pigment bound by gum, to form soft pastels or by oil to form oil pastels. Oil pastels have a rich, luxurious texture, whereas soft pastels have a subtle powdery bloom. Each type of pastel can be mixed with other media, but one of the most expressive combinations is to mix and work the two forms of pastel together. The variations in the surface qualities of opacity and transparency are dependent upon the contrasting adhesive and blending qualities of each type of pastel.

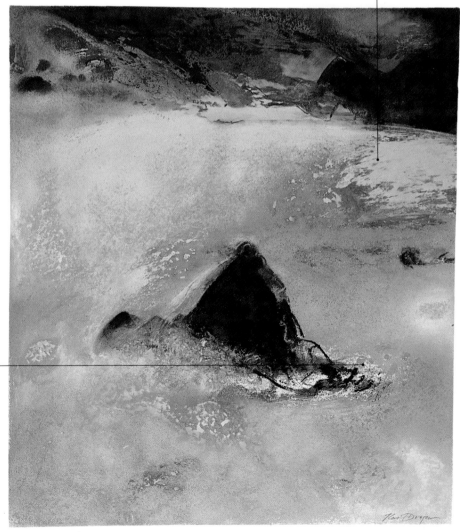

**Combining pastels**

Both of the compositions examined here in detail are the work of a superlative contemporary pastelist. Ken Draper is a British artist and an associate Royal Academician who has extended the expressive potential of soft and oil pastel by using these media in combination. Due to the absence of a liquid medium, soft pastels have the highest degree of luminosity of all the painting media. The expressive power of soft pastels is created by the sensation of pure pigment-reflecting light, but the presence of the oil imparts a

**In this composition** the artist has achieved a luminous evocation of light playing on the contrasting textures of a shoreline. The interactions of light upon water are created by alternating applications of pastel, powdered and blended in a dry wash, and oil pastel, applied in dense impasto.

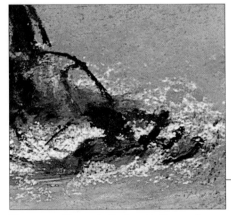

**You can alternate between** line and tone using either the tip or the side of your pastel. The more pressure is applied the more of the medium will be filed away and held by the tooth of the support. The artist has used the texture of the support to create a grainy line in contrast with the smooth blending of the violet tone of the sand.

**Ken Draper, *Recollections,* 1994, oil and soft pastel**

saturated depth of tone to the darker colors. Combining these media creates a visual tension of contrasting degrees of luminosity and surface texture. To achieve the most subtle transitions of tone, a range of similar hues in soft pastels can be crushed into the surface of the support and blended in the manner of a dry wash. In contrast, the artist uses oil pastels to create abrupt passages of bas-relief impasto.

## The physicality of the landscape

A miner's son, Draper shows in his work a heightened awareness of the physical strata of rocks and the power of the landscape. These works are not realistic views but pictorial reconstructions of the forces and substance of earth. Draper's work is characterized by an intense awareness and subtle manipulation of surface qualities both as texture and as a vehicle for color. The elemental forces of nature in the form of matter are reconstituted in an inventive control of pigment that celebrates the interactions of form and light.

**Unlike other painting** media, which are controlled with the aid of brushes and thinners, pastel is generally applied directly onto the surface of the support without any tools. There is a freedom and spontaneity in the directness of pastels that encourages an intensity of involvement in the physical handling. Here, pulling an oil pastel across the raised texture of the support with variable pressure causes it to adhere unevenly, creating a broken surface texture.

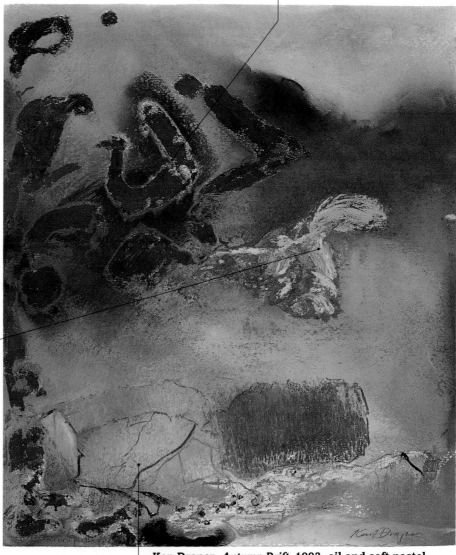

Ken Draper, *Autumn Drift*, 1993, oil and soft pastel

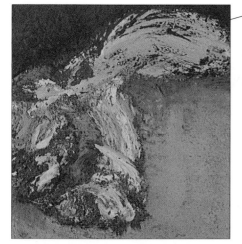

**Oil and soft pastels** have differing degrees of adhesion. The powder of soft pastels can be displaced and blended into the fibers of the support very easily. In contrast, oil pastel vigorously adheres to the support. When dragged, oil pastels become more fluid as they are warmed by the heat of your hand or by the air temperature.

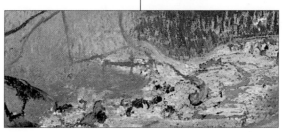

**In this lower** section of the painting, the artist has alternated bold strokes of oil impasto, evoking seaweed, with a subtle blending of soft pastel, overlaid by areas of scumbling and stippling.

# EXPERIMENTING WITH SURFACE

AN EXCITING DIVERSITY of surfaces can be created by using watercolor, gouache, and acrylic paints in combination. Depending on the degree of paint dilution and the texture of the support, you can vary the power of the paint from a transparent wash to a full opaque impasto. Acrylics are designed to work in the widest range of painting techniques, and there are additives that are manufactured to give different qualities of bulk, transparency, or luster to the paint. In addition to the inherent qualities in the paint, there are tools available, including brushes and rollers, that can determine the character of the paint surface.

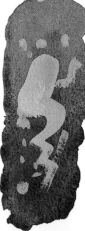

**Broken surface**

*The nature of your support will have a fundamental effect on the surface of the paint. This broken surface effect was made by scraping the paint across a heavily textured paper using a metal painting knife. The paint has been forced into the pitted surface of the support, leaving the raised tooth of the paper free of paint.*

**Gouache impasto**

*Gouache has been applied in impasto over a water-color wash in which two colors were blended wet-into-wet.*

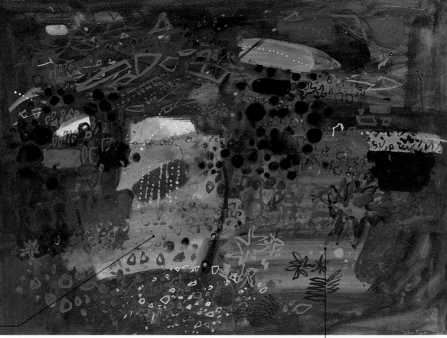

**The renowned** British artist John Piper has engaged in a "tour de force" of texturing and markmaking in this painting. Washes of gray, blue, and green evoke the airy sensations of a landscape in the shadow of dusk against which patterns appear to dance in the space of the composition.

**John Piper, *Landscape,* 1968, watercolor, ink and gouache**

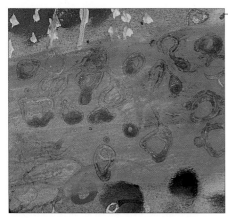

**The surface of the** composition has been built up in successive layers of paint. The orange pattern on the left has been washed over and dispersed into a subtle warm gray wash by mixing with the underlying blue. Blue is the complementary color to orange and on the right-hand, side the artist has superimposed scumbled patches of orange in strident contrast with the underlying turquoise blue.

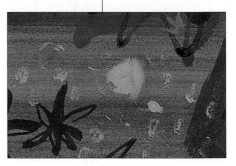

### Creating an illusion

The range of painting techniques, from watercolor washes to opaque mark-making, can also be achieved in acrylic. Whereas Piper has used overlaid washes as a base for a rhythmical counterfoil of irregular and linear marks in gouache and ink, Boyd has capitalized on the properties of acrylic to create areas of dense impasto. Both artists have layered paint, causing the marks to appear to advance and recede as though suspended in space.

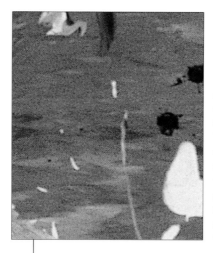

### Texturing with acrylics

This artist engages in an experimental approach exploring the plasticity of acrylics and placing particular emphasis on the rich texturing properties of impasto that can be achieved using this medium. This abstract work was developed from studies of the forces and actions of the sea against coastal rocks that the artist has expressed in an equivalent painterly form through the gestural treatment of the paint surface.

**Areas of deep pink**, ochre, and a tint of ultramarine blue were laid onto a dried gray surface in loose impasto. While the paint was still wet, a large decorator's roller was used to roll the colors across the support. A splash of white paint was then pushed across the surface, and the blunt end of a brush was used to score lines in the pink and ochre sections. Lastly a strip of painted paper was collaged into the wet surface.

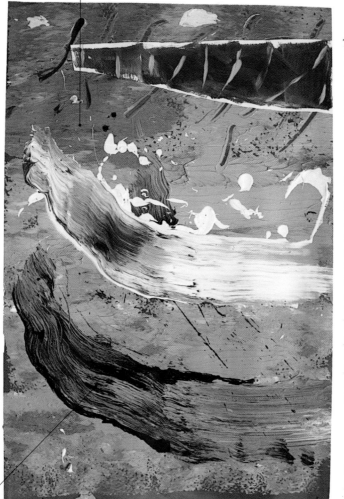

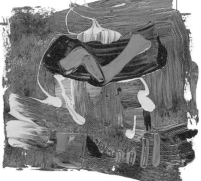

### Wet-into-wet

*Acrylic paint can be worked either wet-into-wet or wet-on-dry. In this example paint has been applied wet-into-wet. Red and yellow have been mixed together to create a rust orange. The colors were worked into each other on the support, and an application of yellow was dribbled and brushed into the orange. Lastly strokes of green and red were laid in single movements to avoid mixing with the underlying colors.*

**Black paint was** laid on the wet surface of the underlying paint, and a large brush was used to pull the fresh application of paint across the surface. A composition that has been worked in impasto will record, in a precise imprint, the actions of the hand, which in turn reflect the thoughts of the artist.

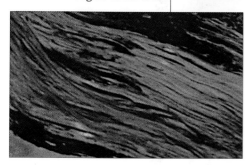

**Graham Boyd, *Untitled* , 1993, acrylic and collage**

### Iridescent acrylics

*Blue acrylic paint has been mixed with gel medium and applied with a painting knife to create a passage of impasto. The paint was allowed to dry, and then a dilution of gold acrylic was applied over the impasto surface to imbue the surface of the blue paint with a metal luster.*

# ADDING TEXTURE

PAINT IS USED PRIMARILY as a coloring medium, but it also has a texture, which can be manipulated in different ways. You can explore an extensive range of surface textures by adding various materials to the paint, including coarse sand, synthetic fibres or even by gluing additional sheets of paper to the support. Irregular textures create a visual disturbance that will significantly affect your perception of the color because of the way the light is reflected from the textured paint surface.

## Choosing your materials

A diversity of texture can be created by using different materials and methods in your composition. You can work onto a uniformly textured ready-made support such as a rough paper or canvas, or create areas of contrasting texture by gluing thin sheets of flexible materials, such as cloth or paper, between the layers of paint as shown here.

The artist has laminated shapes (cut out of sheets of tissue paper) to the support not only to suggest natural forms, but also to intensify the expressive quality of the paint surface of the composition. The creases and edges of the tissue paper have created a heightened sense of surface texture as well as amplifying the feeling of the movement of shapes across the picture surface. By applying tissue paper with PVA glue the paper is turned into a semitransparent film and, after being laid over an existing wash, it will modify the underlying color in the manner of a watercolor.

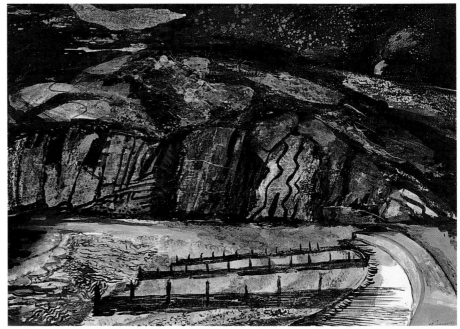

**Craig Peacock, *Rite of Spring*, 1993, mixed media**

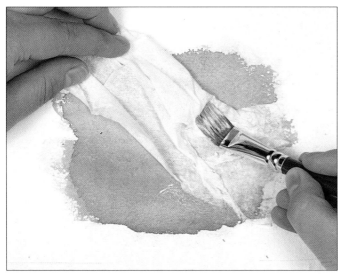

## Using tissue paper and glue

*The textural range of your surface can be changed by laminating tissue paper onto the support using PVA glue. You can either use cut shapes, or fold and corrugate the paper to create a bas-relief surface texture that can be regular and rhythmical or random and erratic.*

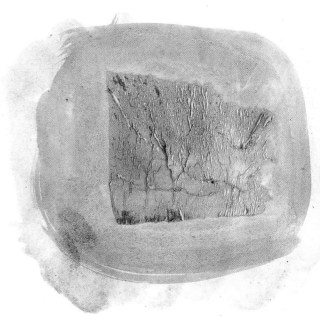

*Once you have glued a sheet of tissue to your support, you can paint over it using any type of paint to emphasize the texture of the tissue.*

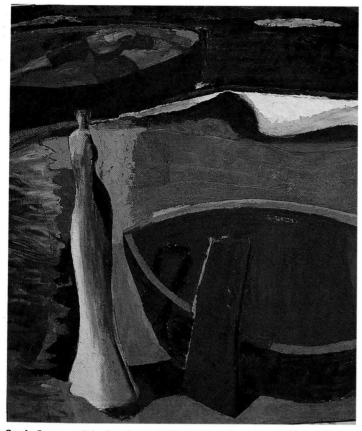

**Sonia Lawson RA,** *Seashore***, 1994, gesso, pigment and linseed paste**

*Powdered pigment*

*Textured gesso*

### Amplifying the surface

Sonia Lawson RA is a painter whose work epitomizes expressive synthesis of color and texture. The physicality of the forms within this enigmatic composition has been amplified by the pronounced granular textural quality in the paint surface. This has been achieved by mixing pigment with linseed paste to produce a more heavily textured paint than those manufactured by artists' color makers and sold in tubes. The textural qualities of the paint surface can also be increased by using a textured gesso that contains carborundum and is sold in different grades of coarseness.

*Linseed paste*

### ADDING TEXTURES

Gesso can be used to create a textured surface or, you can add inert materials such as sand to either the gesso or the paint. Recently some manufacturers have produced textured acrylic media that contain fibers that impart a distinctive irregular texture to the paint.

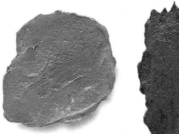

**Fine sand**
*Sands come in different grades from fine to coarse. You can also use a sand that contains different granules to create an uneven texture.*

**Acrylic media**
*Acrylic media contain either granular or stringy fibers. In the example (right) a stringy fiber medium has been added to acrylic color whereas on the left a more granular fiber mixed with turquoise pigment has created a more pronounced texture.*

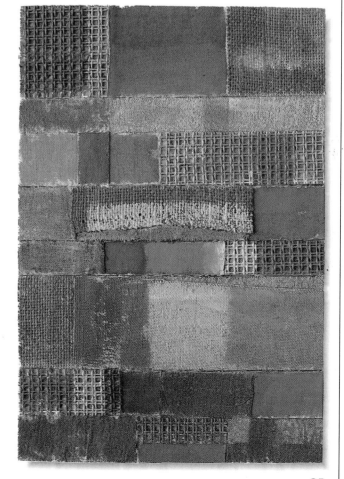

### Color and texture

In this heavily textured composition, the artist has deliberately arranged different collected grades of canvas supports into a pattern of contrasting surface textures. Depending on their degree of intensity and their proximity to a neighboring color, all colors will either advance or recede in the picture space. The use of primary and secondary colors results in the colors pushing and pulling against the surface texture of the collaged materials.

# GESSO AND WAX

A PAINTING IS FIRST and foremost a surface of texture and color. Irrespective of whether a work is abstract or figurative, its power relies on the skill and care with which the surface of the work has been developed. Gesso and wax, used separately or in combination, are two media that produce an interesting array of surface qualities.

Gesso is commonly used to prime a board or canvas in preparation for the application of a paint medium. It is normally applied on an even, flat surface, but it can also be used creatively to develop a bas-relief design within the surface of a composition. Beeswax is a semitransparent medium that produces unique surfaces of paint texture.

GESSO IS AN ANCIENT preparation for priming a painting surface in readiness for paint. Originally gesso was made from chalk and glue, with the addition of small amounts of oil to add flexibility. Manufacturers now produce an excellent modern gesso that is highly flexible and made from acrylic, titanium, and chalk.

## WAX ENCAUSTIC PREPARATION

Wax encaustic is made from beeswax that has been gently melted to a liquid state in a double boiler. This warm wax then has powdered pigment added. The mixture can be used as a medium when the wax is still warm. A little dammar varnish can be added to strengthen the medium. It causes the wax to set on the support within seconds, forming a durable surface.

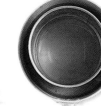
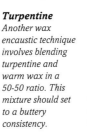
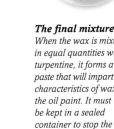

**Solid beeswax**
*Beeswax is one of the oldest painting mediums known – wax paintings have survived since the Egyptians. Wax does not crack, flake, or darken with age.*

**Turpentine**
*Another wax encaustic technique involves blending turpentine and warm wax in a 50-50 ratio. This mixture should set to a buttery consistency.*

**Melting wax**
*Place the wax in a can in a pan of hot water.*

**The final mixture**
*When the wax is mixed in equal quantities with turpentine, it forms a soft paste that will impart the characteristics of wax to the oil paint. It must be kept in a sealed container to stop the wax from hardening.*

**Drawing into gesso**
*A design has been drawn into the surface of the gesso using the end of a brush. You can also add materials to create more texture.*

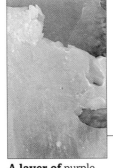

**Applying the wax**
*Here the gesso has had an application of orange wax encaustic scraped across the surface, depositing the color in the indentations.*

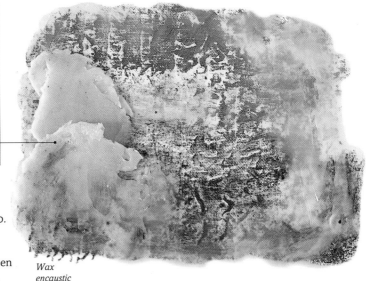

**A layer of** purple and orange wax encaustic has been scraped across gesso. An impasto layer of beeswax without pigment has then been applied with a knife.

*Wax encaustic*

## Texture and geometry

In this powerful composition, the artist has created a beautiful surface using wax over four square panels. The surface was constructed using layers of crepe paper and liquid wax. Afterwards color was added using oil paint and a metallic pigment. The work intends to inspire religious meditation. It was designed to be housed in a large space, with the symbolic positioning of the four squares forming a single square to give the piece a sense of sacred symbolism. The artist has developed a complex textural surface as a source of reverie to complement the severity of the geometry.

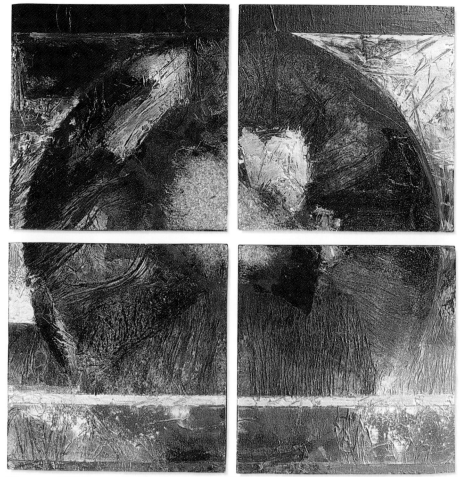

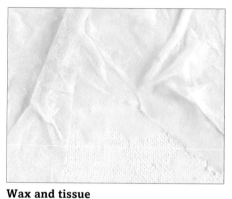

### Wax and tissue

*Poured wax sets in different thicknesses over tissue paper that has been soaked and draped over the surface of the canvas board.*

**Maureen Wilkinson, *Revelation,* 1992, collage and encaustic on wood**

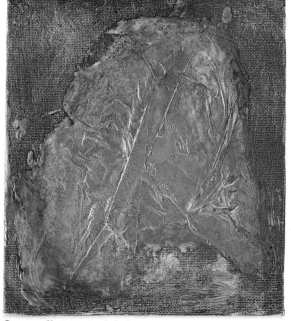

### Suspending materials in wax

*Wax can be used to separate and suspend materials. To create an opaque wax medium, you can apply layers of paint within semitransparent layers of wax or add pigment. Here a sheet of tissue paper was soaked in warm wax. A layer of metallic pigment was brushed into the surface and a thin wash of blue oil paint applied to the surrounding area.*

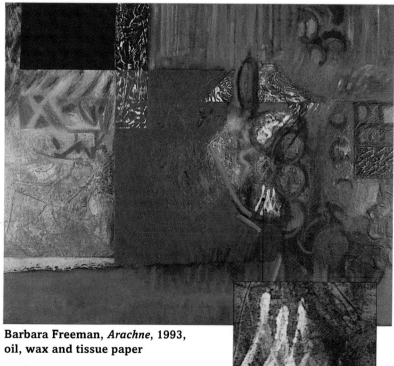

**Barbara Freeman, *Arachne,* 1993, oil, wax and tissue paper**

**The webs** of gesso evoke the myth of Arachne, a weaver who is turned into a spider as revenge by the Greek gods.

37

# UNUSUAL MATERIALS

CONTEMPORARY ARTISTS are often concerned with testing and extending the bounds of visual expression to incorporate unusual materials in the creation of their mixed media compositions. This originality has occurred as artists have searched for materials to fulfill a particular quality of color or texture that is usually outside the scope of more orthodox materials. As a result, the conventional formats have been challenged as artists find alternative shapes to use instead of the familiar rectangle of paper or canvas.

### Using the landscape

Tessa Maiden was raised in a farming community, and her choice of materials and work reflects her awareness of the structure of the landscape. In the two paintings on this page, she has used a highly unusual and inventive arrangement of natural, artificial, regular, and irregular forms. These two pieces were originally part of a vertical arrangement of eight subtly different canvases.

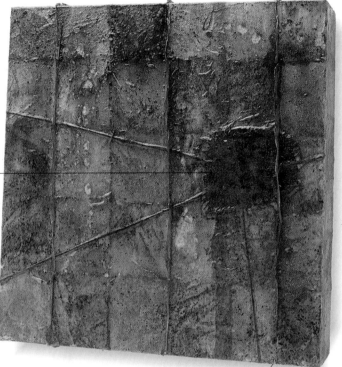

**In contrast with** the regular pattern of the empty tea bags, the artist has created a visual nucleus in each composition by using the contrasting textures of a patch of canvas and radiating lines of string. In the lower half of the canvas, a mixture of button polish and linseed oil has coagulated into patterns on the surface.

**Tessa Maiden,** *Tissue Culture No.1,*
**button polish, tea bags,
linseed oil and string**

### Using tea bags

*The artist has used the tea bags to represent the division of land into fields.*

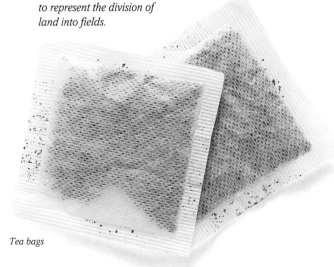

*Tea bags*

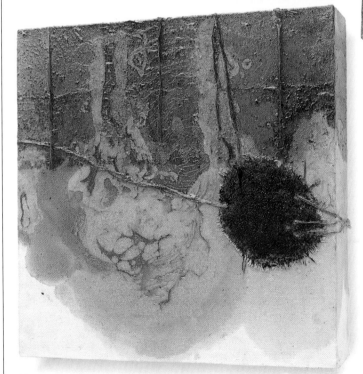

**Tessa Maiden,** *Tissue Culture No.1,*
**button polish, tea bags, linseed oil and string**

## Using metals and wax

The circle is a very pleasing format to work with. Free from the constraints of verticals, horizontals, and right-angled corners, the imagination can explore another world of associations. In this composition, the artist has beaten a thin sheet of copper over a wooden panel and coated the copper surface with a layer of melted wax. The wax was darkened with the addition of pigment, and areas of the impasto wax surface have been scraped away to reveal the uneven texture and reflective surface of the beaten copper.

## The qualities of wax

*Wax is a versatile medium that can be used to alter the qualities of a surface. A light application of wax thinned with turpentine will deepen the tone of wood or stone and will also add transparency to a paper surface.*

**Rowena Dring,**
***Untitled, 1993,***
**tempera, pigment, and wax**

## Using slate

Slate is an ancient building material and would normally be associated with sculpture rather than painting. Here the artist has used slate to create a work that could be defined as a wall sculpture, but whose surface is read in the manner of a painting. A shape that is evocative of land mass has been created by carving into the edges of the slate, then a subtly texturing the surface.

**Rowena Dring,**
***Diskworld,*** **slate and plastic padding**

*Natural slate*

# GALLERY OF PAINTING

PAINTINGS CREATED BEFORE the 20th century were largely figurative – using artistic conventions such as perspective, they offered convincing pictures of the world as we knew it. Contemporary art is often more abstract, emphasizing colors, shapes and textures, which results in more attention being focused on the picture surface itself. This has resulted in an extraordinary period of experimentation in which artists have used a huge range of materials to produce an exciting array of mixed media works. Artists have concentrated on generating a new awareness of surface and have succeeded by adding materials, by using impasto techniques, and by scraping and inscribing a surface to amplify the characteristics of each medium.

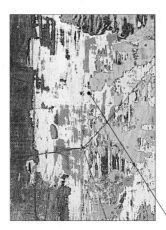

**Nicholson has** used an unusual vertical, double square format for this large canvas. He has worked the surface in colors and textures that are similar to weathered stone. A definite structure of shapes within the piece complements the diffuse texture of the paint surface. The finely scraped layers of gray paint reveal previous applications of color and create the sense of an underlying strucure being rediscovered.

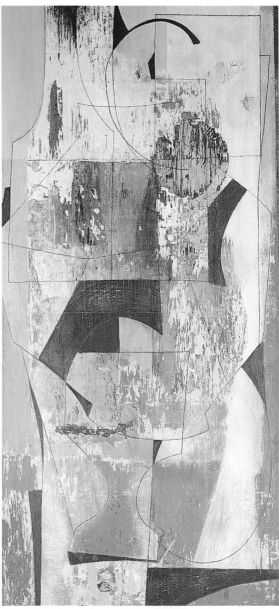

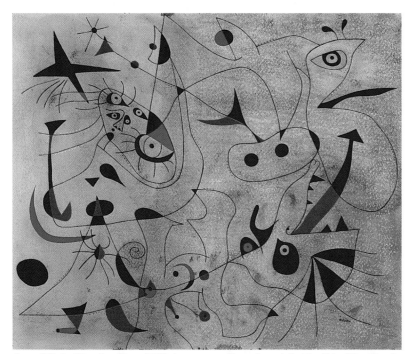

**Joan Miró,** *Morning Star,* **1940, tempera, oil, and pastel** *15 x 18 in (38 x 46 cm)*
*Joan Miró (1893–1983) was one of the major Surrealists, and here he employs a perennial surrealist device – the juxtaposition of incongruous subjects to disturb our normal perception. In this piece, Miró demonstrates the combination of wet and dry painting materials by rubbing pastel into the support to amplify the texture of the surface and contrast with the opaque painted shapes. A menagerie of beasts linked by a linear framework forms a dreamlike constellation that floats against the nebulous vapors implied by the pastel wash. Miró was profoundly influenced by his Catalan roots, as shown by his strident patterns and his inventive use of textured materials.*

**Ben Nicholson,** *August 1952 (Palimpsest),* **(detail) oil and pencil** *42 x 21 in (107 x 53 cm)*
*A "palimpsest" is a piece of paper or parchment on which the original text has been obliterated to make room for other writing. Nicholson has built up subtle layers of paint by wiping and then scraping back the pigment on a textured surface.*

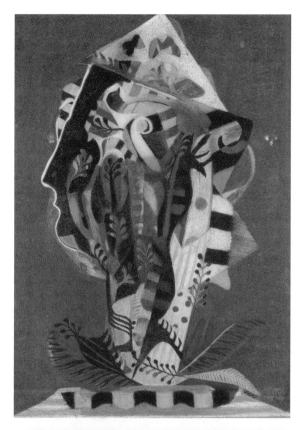

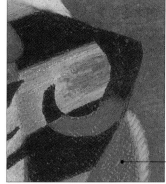

**Agar has taken meticulous** care in the organization of the design by manipulating pastel in careful transitions to retain the purity and saturation of the colors. Particular attention has been given to the edge of the forms to achieve distinct shapes. There is a careful avoidance of casual gesture and a deliberate flattening of shapes into silhouettes.

**Eileen Agar, *Orpheus*, 1991, pastel and chalk**
*33 x 24 in (84 x 61 cm)*
*Eileen Agar's use of vibrant colored chalks and pastels evokes the beguiling power of music and prompts an imaginative reading of the head in profile as the entrance to an underworld of dreams. The image, imbued with a visual lyricism and the inventive use of organic shapes, evokes a pastoral theme.*

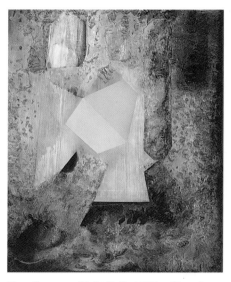

**Ken Draper, *Light Fall,* 1993, oil and pigment on wood** *48 x 42 in (122 x 107 cm)*
*In this startling mixed media composition, the artist has employed an innovative combination of oil paints with pure pigment in powder form. The wood grain has been stained using oil paint to emphasize the support. Rectilinear shapes have been delineated in masking tape. Draper has created extremes of texture by blending pigment into the smooth surface of the wooden panel as a foil to the bas-relief surface in oil paint. The painting is a compelling allusion to the structure of the earth's crust.*

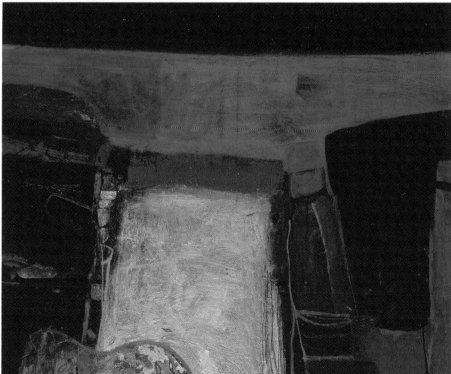

**The artist has scraped** through the layer of gold in a sgraffito technique to create an inscribed pattern of foliage. The allusion to vegetation has been amplified by the use of a Viridian green that has been glazed over the gold. This detailing highlights the monumental scale of the towering gold edifice.

**Barbara Rae, *Field Altandhu*, 1994, oil or acrylic with gold paint** *67 x 76 in (170 x 194 cm)*
*In this large-scale work, the artist has evoked an exotic night through a sumptuous combination of iridescent gold pigment and saturated colors. The surface of the support has been textured and reworked in layers of pigment that can be seen in the shimmering surface of the area in gold. The deep blue unifies the broken surface and throws the iridescent gold and luminous red band into high relief.*

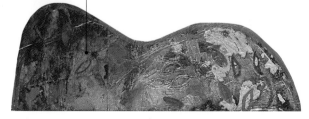

# COLLAGE MATERIALS

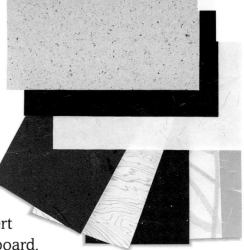

COLLAGE, LIKE ANY OTHER ART FORM, needs to be held together with a visual theme, either by a dominant color, an emphasis on contrasting textures, or a linking concept such as landscape. Once you have established a theme, you can experiment with collaging almost any inert material that you can stick to a sheet of paper or a board. Any light material such as plastic or cloth can be attached to a heavyweight paper support using glue. Heavier wood and metal materials are best attached to a stronger support of either a board or panel.

THERE IS AN INEXHAUSTIBLE wealth of colored and textured materials to be found for collaging, including, tissue papers, newspaper imagery, magazines, posters, books, wallpaper, packing materials, and cardboard. An experienced collagist soon learns that "junk" can be rearranged to form a compelling artwork and develops the habit of collecting and storing found materials to form a storehouse of stimuli for the imagination. Suitable materials for bas-relief collages are light metal sheeting, aluminum foil, thin plywood, and veneers. You can also use flexible linear materials like string and wire to add curvilinear shape to your composition.

The average home is a great source of materials, not only for the wide selection of disposable cardboard, plastic, and paper that accumulates in the home, but also for the range of dried foods to be found in the kitchen, such as grains, beans, and pastas. However, it is important to use only food materials that will not disintegrate when exposed to the air.

**Printed material**

*Newspapers, magazines, and brochures provide a surfeit of disposable printed material and imagery. The fonts and scales of the letter forms are particularly useful.*

**Old photographs**

*Most vacations and events result in a number of unwanted photographs. These can be filed into subjects and used to form collages on different themes, and they can also inspire a color theme.*

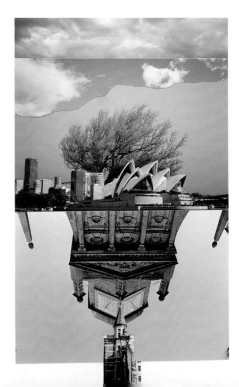

**Assorted fabrics**

*The delightful and seemingly endless diversity of natural and synthetic fabrics is highly suitable for collage. Fabrics can be grouped and organized in a composition according to texture and color. You may wish to begin with contrasting patterns of printed cotton or the different weaves and textures of canvas and burlap.*

*Burned tin can*

### Found objects

*Discarded items and broken household appliances can be dismantled to retrieve small machine parts that inspire ideas. Complex electrical parts, along with broken toys, provide a ready supply of diverse shapes and forms that can suggest themes to explore in collage.*

*Glue gun & glue sticks*

*Discarded toys & shapes*

*Copper wire*

*Pumice stone*

*Tinfoil pie-case*

*Wood glue*

*PVA glue*

### Found natural objects

*A walk through a garden will provide many natural, beautifully textured leaves, twigs, seeds, grasses, and barks, which are very suitable for collaging. Beaches are good hunting grounds for artists, and works can be developed from weathered fragments of rope, driftwood, and stones. The beauty of these fragments is that they are textured from the action of the sea.*

### Adhesives

*For light paper and fabric materials a PVA glue is ideal. There is a range of wood glues that are suitable for plywood, veneers, and driftwood, but they take some time to dry. A helpful tool for bas-relief collage is an electric glue gun, which heats the glue and squeezes it through a nozzle onto the support. This is particularly useful for metal and stone.*

*Found objects*

### Cutting implements

*Paper and cardboard are quickly cut to shape using either a sharp craft knife or a pair of scissors. A useful addition to your tool kit is a pair of wire cutters which can cut thin sheets of metal and mesh.*

### Fretsaw

*The fretsaw is a saw that is designed to allow for the cutting of complex shapes from thin sheets of wood. The thin saw blade is held in tension and can easily cut and form curves.*

*Wire cutters*

# PRINTING MATERIALS

PRINTMAKING MAY SEEM a forbidding prospect, requiring access to presses and a printmaking studio. However, it is possible to create a range of fascinating and creative prints without the necessity for expensive machinery. Printing is basically the process of lifting an impression from a surface that has been inked or, instead, pressing painted shapes onto a paper surface. There are many materials that are suitable for printmaking. It is a simple process to develop works of striking texture and color using inexpensive tools.

*Wooden spoon*

*Palette knife*

THE MOST POPULAR method of creating a print is by relief printmaking. This involves either cutting into or building up a printing surface into a pattern of raised shapes. Ink is then rolled over the surface of the printing block and a sheet of smooth paper placed on the inked surface. Even pressure is then applied to transfer the design onto the paper. Pressure is best applied by either using a roller or rubbing the back of a wooden spoon across the back of the paper. Another highly creative process for you to explore is monoprint. This involves painting a design onto a sheet of smooth impermeable material such as acetate or glass. Again, make a print by rubbing the back of the paper with a roller or spoon.

*Roller with ink*

## Ink and surfaces

*Inks should be mixed with a spatula on a palette of either plate glass or, as a safer alternative, a sheet of acetate or plastic. The ink should be taken up with a roller, which should lift enough ink to coat the printing block evenly. As you roll, you can control the thickness of the ink to create either a transparent or opaque application.*

## Masking out

*Masking tape is designed for blocking out areas of a composition before an application of paint or ink. The tape is then peeled away from the surface, allowing the underlying tone to show through. Masking tape is also essential for securing the paper to prevent movement when making a print.*

## Brushes

*Different-sized brushes are used in monotype printing to apply and move the ink around on the plate, creating areas of line or tone. Brushes are also used as an alternative to the uniform application achieved by rollers.*

## Scalpel

*Scalpels are useful for carving patterns into sheets of paper and card for printing.*

## Printing inks

*Printing inks are made of finely ground pigments suspended in a transparent drying medium. Inks come in an extensive range of colors, but by mixing the three primary colors of magenta, cyan, and yellow, along with black and white, you can create a full palette of colors. Most commercial inks are oil based and are thinned with mineral spirits. You can also buy water-based inks. Manufacturers make an extending medium for oil-based inks that can be added to create transparent tints.*

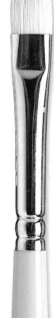

### Shellac

*Shellac is a resin-based varnish. It can be used to seal the surface of a bas-relief work or collagraph. The dried application of shellac stops the cardboard from absorbing water- and oil-based inks. Without the layer of shellac, the surface of a bas-relief cardboard print will deteriorate in contact with the ink, allowing only a few impressions to be taken.*

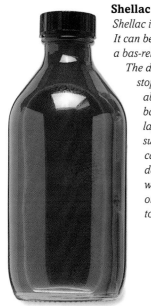

*Shellac*

*Rubber stamp*

*Positive and negative card cutouts*

*A piece of jigsaw puzzle*

*Plasticine mold*

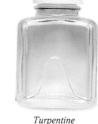

*Turpentine*

*Plasticine mold*

### Linseed oil and turpentine

*Linseed oil is used as an extending medium for printing ink and oil paint and will increase the transparency of the colors. Turpentine is used to clean the roller after a printing session.*

*Linseed Oil*

### Printing blocks

*Cardboard is easily cut with a craft knife or scissors to form a printing block. Rigid shapes can also be cut from hardboard or plywood using a fretsaw. Other more easily cut materials include balsa wood and polystyrene. You can also take impressions from surfaces using plasticine, which can then be used as a short-term printing block.*

*Wooden stamp*

### Variety of textures

*There is a wide selection of synthetic materials that can be either cut or crumpled to create a textured surface. Each material is capable of different patterns by either folding to create regular creases or crumpling to create irregular patterns in the folds. There are other interesting textures in products that have been made with a bas-relief surface, such as certain wallpapers, bubble wrap, and woven fibers.*

*Plastic wrap*

*Aluminum foil*

### Using found objects

*Collagraphs can be made from a diversity of materials, including string and thin wire, which are ideal for creating curved lines. These shapes can be used in contrast with the more regular weaves of gauze and other heavily textured fabrics. Grains such as rice can be used to create a pattern of small marks.*

*Bubble wrap*

*Tracing paper*

# COLOR COLLAGE

COLLAGE IS A TECHNIQUE of cutting and arranging colored or toned materials to form a composition of shapes. This allows for extensive exploration of possible arrangements and affords scope for many adjustments before fixing the shapes in place. A major advantage of collage is that you can build an arrangement rapidly, which encourages a confident and inventive treatment. A color collage also makes an excellent base for additional mixed media techniques using paint and found objects.

### Using your sketches

The artist has developed a dynamic compositional theme based on life drawings of the figure in motion. The implications of translating the drawing into collage are that the shape becomes the sole means of expression as the process of collage reduces the figure to flat shapes. The artist has selected angular and curved shapes from his sketches to emphasize movement.

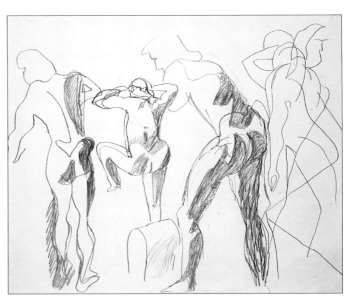

### A collection of sketches

By placing a number of studies on the same sheet, interactions of positive and negative shapes occur, acting as a prompt to the imagination.

1 ◀ The artist has carefully transferred selected shapes from his drawing onto hand-colored sheets of paper and cut around the outline using a pair of scissors. The sheets were prepared using a large brush to apply a quick-drying wash of acrylic. An alternative is to buy a selection of already colored sheets from paper suppliers who sell a wide spectrum of colored sheets specifically designed for collage.

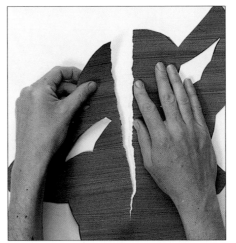

2 ◀ The dominant concern of collage is forming and arranging expressive shapes. As a means of intensifying the character of the shapes, the artist has chosen to vary the texture of the edges of the forms by alternating between the sharp edge of a shape cut with scissors and the ragged edge created by tearing the paper.

# NEGATIVE SPACE

Composition is profoundly affected by having to translate a three-dimensional world of forms onto a two-dimensional surface. This process creates new shapes in the subject, but they only come into existence on the picture surface. They are the negative shapes that are created between the positive form of the subject and other areas of the composition. The negative shapes are as important as the positive shapes, and it is in collage that this awareness of composition can be most fully developed to create a a range of interesting images.

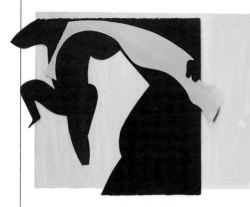

### Maximum effect
*The cut shapes have been shifted in this collage arrangement until the maximum interaction between the positive cut shapes and the negative shapes of the remaining areas of the support has been achieved.*

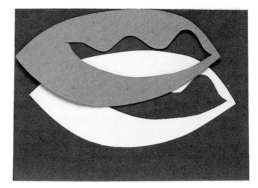

### Overlapping
*The original leaf design has been transformed into a complex interaction of positive and negative shapes by the simple process of overlapping.*

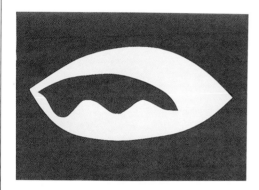

### Scale and format
*It is vital to consider the relationship between the position of the positive shape and the scale and format of the support. Here the shape is placed in an uninteresting static position, creating no interaction.*

### Positioning the shapes
*The positive white shapes have been carefully positioned to touch the edge of the support and each other, creating dynamic negative red shapes among the positive shapes.*

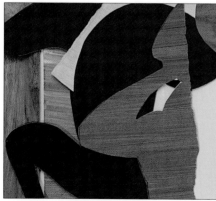

3 ▲ Where the shapes overlap, contrasting areas of primary and secondary color create a tension of positive and negative shapes in the composition.

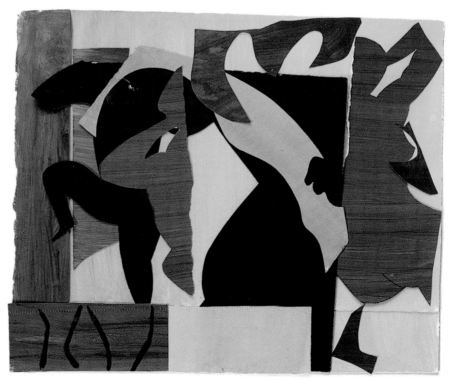

## Making connections
In the final composition there are two movements leading the eye through the artwork in different ways – through the recurrence of curved lines and the repetition of colors, which create alternative sets of connections.

# PHOTO-COLLAGING

COLLAGING PHOTOGRAPHIC IMAGERY has become a mainstream contemporary art form that is both a product and mirror of our technological age. Technology now provides us with a perpetually renewed fund of ready-made printed imagery in the form of magazines, advertising, posters, and newspapers. We also create personal imagery using our own cameras. The essential principle of collage is the arrangement of cut shapes on an esthetic or a conceptual theme. Imagery for the collage can also be manipulated by using either a photocopier or a computer.

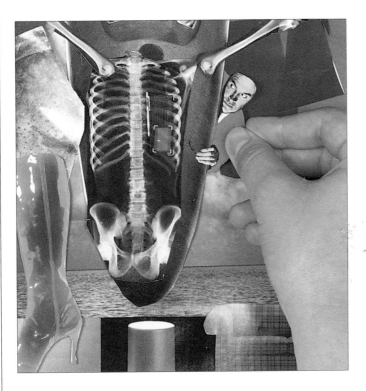

*A selection of cut out images*

### Choosing a theme

Through selection and organization, collaging can result in powerful contrasting visual qualities of form. This can be seen here in the surreal photographic montage by Ed Smy. The artist's working method is to select and store imagery by themes – for example, machines, organic forms, and faces. The stored images are used as a fund of potential collage imagery. This collage was created by carefully arranging areas of color to create a dominant color key and a stage-like illusion of space. As a sculptor, Ed Smy is interested in the expressive power of combining familiar forms in a new context.

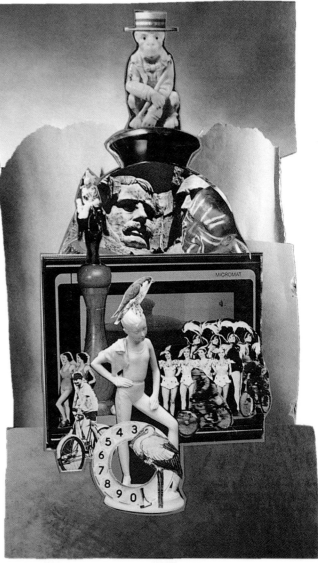

### Composing your collage

Collage can be used to draw images from our unconscious and to create compositions that reflect the incongruous juxtapositions that confront us daily. In the home, magazines and television flood our minds with imagery. In the street, billboards jostle for attention among the multitudes of items displayed in store windows. This bombardment of visual stimuli gives modern life a surreal quality that is strikingly mirrored by this witty collage.

**Ed Smy** *Vaudeville, 1994,* **photo-collage**

### Reduction and enlargement

The photocopier has given the contemporary artist exciting new effects to exploit in collage. New artistic possibilities are generated through the ease with which these machines reduce and enlarge printed imagery in both color and monotone. The photocopier, like all print forms, has its own particular quality of tone and texture, exaggerating the tone to either black or white.

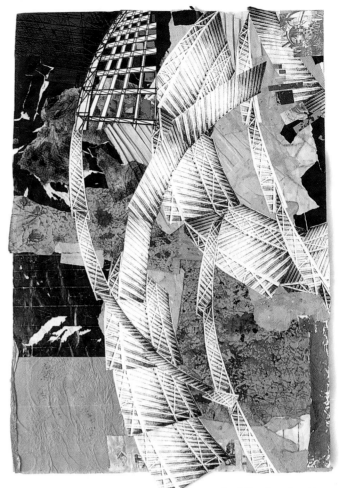

### Creating symmetry

In this unusual arrangement, an image has been repeated and cut into irregular shapes. The cropped image of the front of a building has been given a new reading as a symmetrical abstract design of black and white textured shapes.

### Architectural patterns

In this collage, the artist has used a photocopier to enlarge and reduce original photographs to the scale necessary for the composition. Images of architectural structure have been repeated and collaged over textured and painted papers to create an inventive painting.

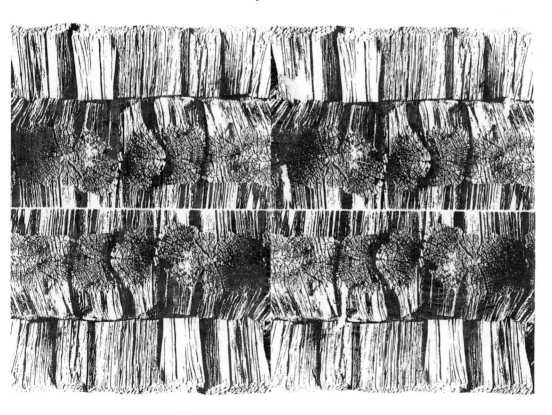

### Repeat patterns

Any image can be constructed into a repeat pattern within minutes, allowing the artist to make rapid decisions and significant changes without difficulty. Here, a photograph of heavily textured stacks of wood has been repeated, using four sheets to create a single composition. It can also work as a textile design.

# HANDMADE PAPER

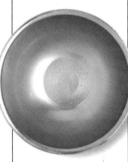

*Mixing bowl*

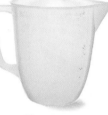

*Measuring cup*

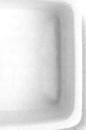

*Plastic bowl*

*Shredded paper*

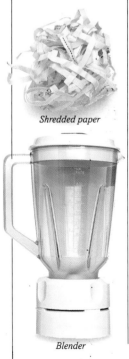

*Blender*

MAKING YOUR OWN PAPER is a surprisingly simple process and a useful skill to master for creating unusual mixed media pieces. A number of qualities of surface can only be created by making your own paper. To do this you will need to buy some basic materials including a mold and deckle, which is a fine mesh stretched over a frame to catch a thin layer of pulp. The simple process of soaking and shredding existing paper into a pulp can allow you to create a raw mixture that you can work in many ways. You can either add pigments or dyes to create color or blend in a range of other fibers.

### Making your own paper

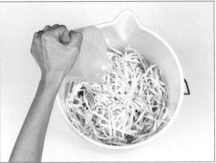

**1 ▲** Tear up old paper and place the shreds in a bucket. Add enough hot water to make sure you fully submerge all the paper. Leave the paper to soak for at least an hour or, ideally, overnight.

**2 ▶** The presoaked paper mixture needs to be pureed to reduce it to a pulp. This can be done in an ordinary blender in about 30 seconds. If you want to create a coarse pulp, puree for only 10–15 seconds in short bursts.

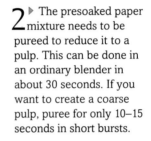

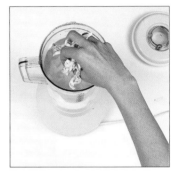

**3 ◀** Fill a plastic bowl half full with tepid water and pour in the pulp mixture from the blender. A half-full bowl of water should only take one load of pulp. Stir the mixture to disperse the pulp.

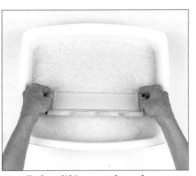

**4 ▲** Before lifting out the pulp you should prepare a board by placing felts over wet newspaper laid over a wooden board. Submerge the mold and deckle into the mixture, mesh side up, at a 45° angle.

**5 ▶** It is important to get an even covering of pulp on the mesh. The mold and deckle should then be lifted out horizontally, allowing the excess water to drain off.

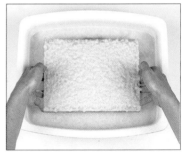

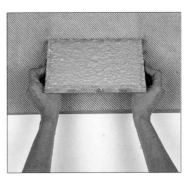

**6 ◀** Making sure the prepared surface is very even and moist, quickly flip the mold and deckle over and place the frame face down onto the felt.

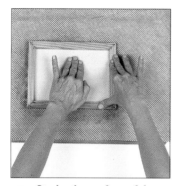

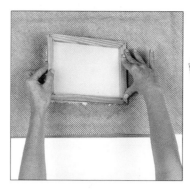

**Materials**

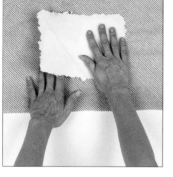

*Felts*

**8** ▶ It is extremely important to bounce off the mold and deckle in a quick clean movement. This is done by holding one end firmly and bouncing off the opposite side. This should leave the layer of pulp on the board.

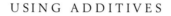

**7** ▲ Stroke the surface of the mesh to sponge off some of the excess liquid and flatten the pulp onto the felt. You can build up layers of paper by placing a wet felt between each layer of pulp.

**9** ◀ The pulp should be left to dry into sheets of paper. This can be done by leaving the layers of pulp to dry together in a pile or by taking each piece of felt and hanging it up to dry on a line. The paper should only take a couple of hours to dry into a sheet. Once dry, the paper should be carefully peeled off and sealed using starch, gelatin, or PVA glue.

*Mold and deckle*

## USING ADDITIVES

### Natural additives

Give interest and texture to your paper by adding all kinds of material to the paper pulp, ranging from dried grasses, leaves, petals, seeds, and thin bark to different grades of textured and colored papers, threads, cottons, string, and nylon netting. There are different ways in which you can add your collected materials to the prepared paper pulp. You can break up plant and paper fibers by pureeing them into your paper pulp. This will create flecks of various colors and textures in the paper. This is an excellent method for creating sheets of paper of a uniform texture with subtle variations of color. The size of the additional fibers can be varied by the amount of shredding the fibers undergo in the blender and you can create a

*Natural objects*

surface with more contrast by blending in larger fibers or simply by pressing material such as small petals into the surface of a sheet of wet pulp. You can make some very unusual papers out of a range of plant fibers such as the leaves of the iris plant, which can be used as an alternative to paper pulp. The cellulose in the leaves needs to be broken down first by soaking the leaves in a solution of sodium hydroxide and then washing the fibers to remove any trace of chemicals. The fibers are then blended and pressed in the same manner as other pulps.

### Laminating

Laminating is a process that involves pressing long fibers such as string and netting between two or more layers of wet pulp. This method of constructing paper allows you to experiment, creating some very original shapes. You can either sandwich the string between two layers of paper pulp or use the string or netting as a structure on which to press broken areas of pulp into irregular shapes.

*String and coloured threads*

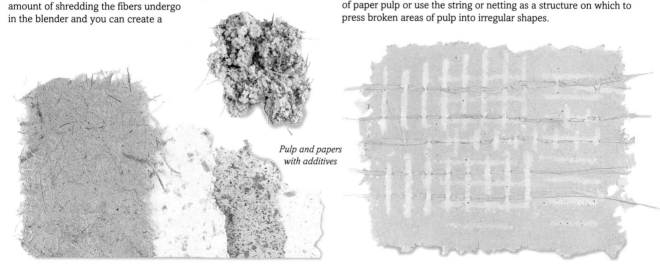

*Pulp and papers with additives*

# CREATING AN IMAGE IN PAPER

HAVING EXPLORED THE PROCESS of making paper, you can now adapt this technique to create your own imagery. The raw pulp can be colored most effectively by adding dyes, but you can also use water-based paint. The different colors of pulp can then be manipulated into shapes to form a composition of varied areas of color. An excellent way to create an image in your handmade paper is to use sheets of aluminum mesh (available where autoparts are sold and in some hardware stores) that can be cut into templates and used to create precise shapes of color.

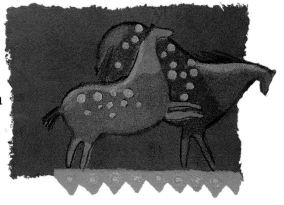

*Handmade paper overworked with crayons and paints*

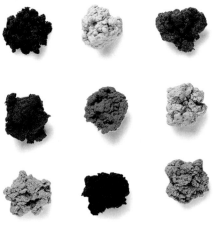

*Colored pulps*

TO CREATE AN exciting image using handmade papers, you can experiment by overlaying complex arrangements of different colors and textures of pulp and later rework the surface of the dry paper with different materials. The design of your sheet of handmade paper can be as simple or intricate as you desire. The piece above uses different colors of pulp for the basic shape of the horses and then uses gold pastels and paint to create the highlights and embossed patterns.

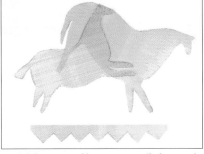

1 ▲ Make yourself some stencils by cutting fine aluminum mesh into your chosen shape. It is important to choose your shapes carefully and to practice some layouts before you start.

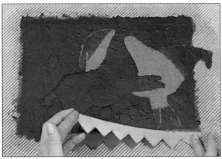

2 ▲ Place your chosen color of base layer onto the prepared board. Submerge the stencil in a different color of pulp, then place the shape on the base layer and lift off in the usual way.

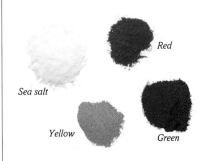

3 ▲ After you have created the basic layout, you can add highlights to the images by simply submerging small areas of the stencils in contrasting colors of pulp and placing these on top.

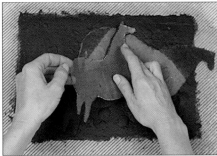

4 ▲ You can use any shape of stencil to build up your image, and you can add many subtle variations of color. Leave the pulp to dry in the usual way before applying any other media.

## DYEING PULP

To dye pulp ideally you should use procion dyes. Place two handfuls of strained paper in a saucepan. Add one gallon of water, a cup of salt as a fixing agent, half a cup of household soda, which helps the pulp absorb the dye, and a cup of dye. Simmer for 10 minutes over a low heat. Rinse the pulp in cold water and put it through a strainer to ensure that the color will not bleed out of the pulp. You can keep the dyed pulps for future use by sealing them in bags and storing them in a refrigerator.

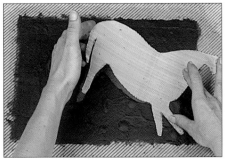

Red

Sea salt

Yellow

Green

## Working with handmade papers

Working with handmade papers is very satisfying, since the addition of color pigments emphasizes the color and texture of the paper. You can exploit the texture of the paper surface using a selection of dry drawing and painting media. A light application of charcoal or soft pastels will leave a grainy textured area of pigment through which the color of the paper will sparkle. Oil pastels have a stickier quality, and you can experiment melting the pastels into the paper using a warm iron on a sheet of paper placed over the work. It is also worth experimenting with blades, sandpaper, and steel wool to scratch through the layers of pigment. An interesting way of removing the color of the dye in the paper and of any other subsequent application of ink is to use household bleach to take out the color and leave a faded white pattern on the surface. You can work the surface of the paper even more by tearing and cutting additional pieces of paper and gluing these and other light objects, such as feathers and string, to the surface. You can also print patterns on the surface using painted shapes of cardboard and plastic erasers.

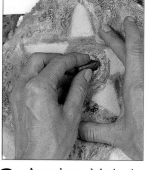

*Various handmade colored papers*

## Building up color

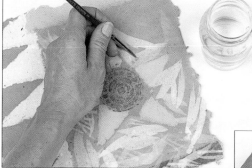

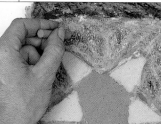

1 ◄ Once finished a piece of patterned handmade paper can be overworked using a variety of media. In this piece the artist starts by using bleach to produce white marks on the paper.

2 ▶ This particular piece has been overworked using soft pastels and crayons of various colors, but you can overwork your paper with any kind of media you find suitable.

3 ▲ An embossed design is created in the center of the star by rubbing a metallic pastel over a textured surface. Here the artist has used a patterned wooden board for the rubbing.

### Materials

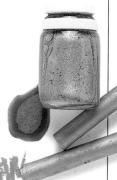

*Steel wool*

*Gold crayons and paint*

*Wax crayons*

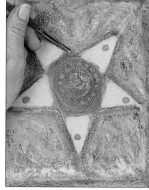

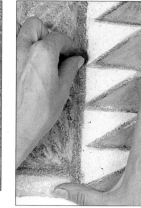

4 ▲ The metallic wax crayon can be overworked and emphasized using gold poster paint or gouache.

5 ▲ The distressed effect is created by scratching off areas of the crayon and paint with steel wool.

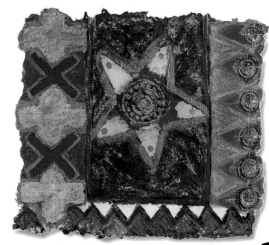

*This piece shows the level to which these handmade papers can be overworked using a variety of different techniques.*

*Brush and bleach*

# COLLAGE-LAMINATE & FROTTAGE

FROTTAGE IS THE TECHNIQUE of taking a rubbing from a textured surface. These rubbings can be developed into sophisticated designs by collaging the different patterns into a composition. Laminating is an extension of collage. It is produced by gluing thin sheets of tissue paper together, which effectively causes the sheets to become transparent layers of color. These two techniques can be explored and used together.

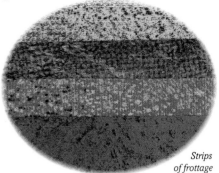

*Strips of frottage*

TO CREATE A FROTTAGE, the side of a wax crayon or chalk is rubbed evenly across a thin sheet of paper placed over the surface of any textured form. This process can be developed into complex layers of patterns by taking a rubbing of a surface and then using the same sheet to take a rubbing from another surface. There is a multitude of patterns to be found, including wall and floor surfaces, grid patterns on metal castings, and the bark of trees. A collection of patterns can be employed as a palette of textures for future collages.

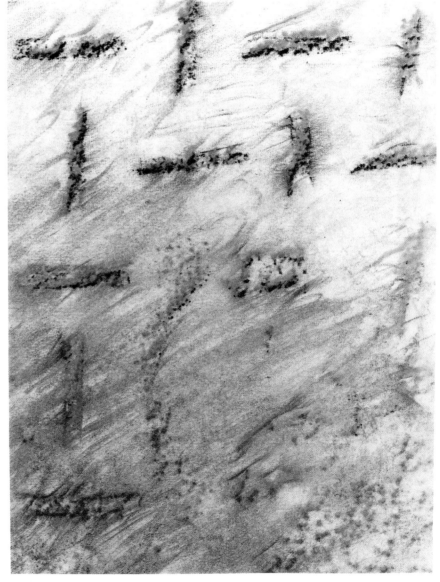

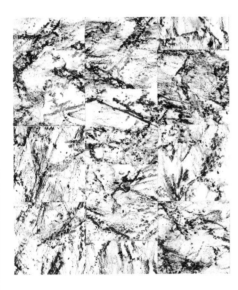

**Composing with patterns**
You can overlay different patterns of the same or contrasting colors using a wax crayon, an oil pastel, or a water-soluble pastel. You can also take a rubbing and then shift the paper to another angle and take another rubbing so that the overlaid rubbing runs in a direction counter to the first impression. Intriguing and dynamic designs can be composed by cutting the frottaged sheets into shapes and placing the different textured areas into a composition, thus capitalizing on the contrasting textures and directions of the marks.

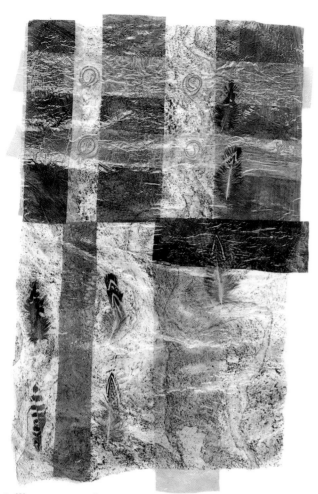

## Laminating paper step-by-step

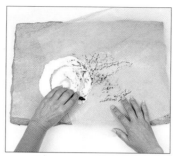

**1** ▲ Place tissue paper over your chosen textured surface and rub with the side of a wax crayon or pastel to reveal a pattern. You can also use white and metallic crayons on colored paper.

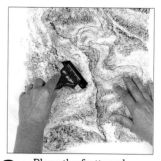

**2** ▲ Place the frottaged tissue over a sheet of plain tissue that has been coated with diluted PVA glue. Flatten out the paper using a printmaking roller.

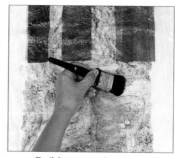

**3** ▲ Build up your laminated frottage using different pieces of tissue paper. You can use store-bought colored tissue or create your own colors by using washes of thinned acrylic paint on top of each glued layer.

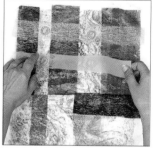

**4** ▲ A variety of objects can be added to the laminating process, including string (coiled into shapes) and metallic papers. Simply place them onto the paper and paste another sheet on top.

### Detailing your work

The artist has contrasted the delicate monochrome rhythms of the frottage by laminating additional bands of a darker tone and colored string and feathers into the surface of the composition.

### Working onto your lamination

Here the artist has created a *"tour de force,"* exploring the possibilities of combining frottage and lamination. Frottaging has been used to lift a pattern from the weathered surface of a stone, creating a snakelike movement through the composition. Sheets of tissue paper have been prepared by painting on patterns of bleach with a brush, thereby bleaching out the color of the paper.

Patterns have been printed onto tissue paper using corrugated cardboard. The overlaid sheets of tissue paper have been transformed by the diluted washes of PVA into transparent veils of color that contrast with the opaque forms of the feathers and string embedded between the tinted layers of tissue paper. Another way to develop your laminated frottage is to use an oil-based medium for the frottage and overlay a wash of watercolor on top. This will create a striking resist technique.

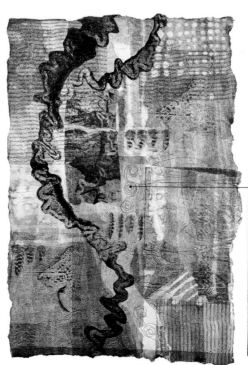

### Creating details

The ochre tissue paper creates a golden glow that contrasts with the texture of the stone design and twists of string. Ink from a fresh photocopy can be transferred onto another sheet by placing the photocopy face down, dampening the back with a solution of detergent, water, and solvent and then rubbing hard.

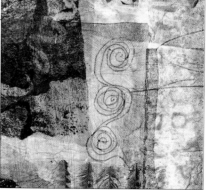

# BAS-RELIEFS

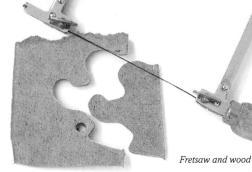

*Fretsaw and wood*

THE VISUAL QUALITIES required for a good collage are shape, tone, color, and texture. As you start to use materials with a more pronounced texture, you will inevitably begin to explore bas-relief form. You can create these forms out of cardboard, wood, and paper. Paper is a highly versatile medium and not immediately associated with bas-relief, but it can be used to create striking bas-relief forms by cutting, folding, gluing, and weaving. There is also a diversity of suitable bas-relief materials provided by objects found in nature and the discarded products of a consumer society.

*Found objects*

A BAS-RELIEF COLLAGE requires a unifying theme and so simply by using the right natural objects you can produce harmonies of textures and forms. You can see the natural harmony in the common characteristics of weathered fragments such as driftwood, rope, bits of corroded metals and plastics. In addition to collecting materials, you can develop bas-relief works in prepared wood, sheets of cardboard, plywood, and hardboard. You can then paint and stain them to form a colored bas-relief composition. Thin wood can be sawed into complex shapes using a fretsaw and glued in place using a glue gun.

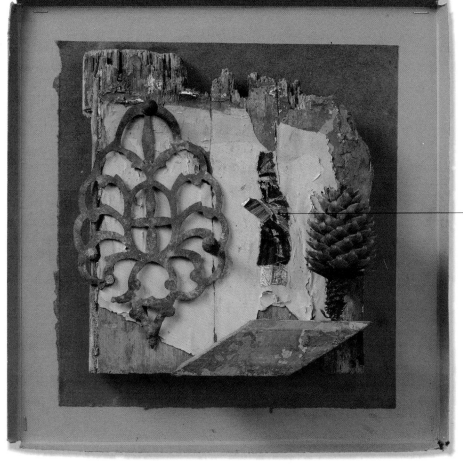

**The intense hot** colors of the base of the work amplify the enclosed green area, giving this space the impression of verdant coolness and calm. The scale of the paper figure forces the fir cone and the metal cast to be reread as ornamental bushes. This inventive use of materials epitomizes the creative skill of making a prosaic object appear poetic by allowing the object to evoke other forms.

**Dick Lee, RA, *In a Persian Garden*, 1994, found object collage**

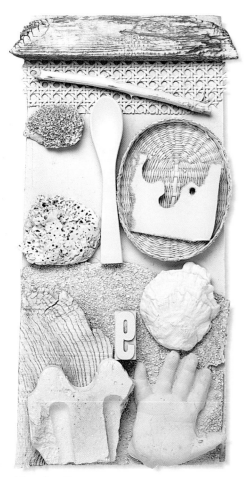

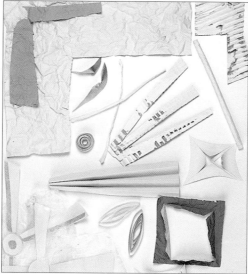

### Weaving paper
*You can either use a single type of paper or alternate different-toned and textured papers as you weave the strips together.*

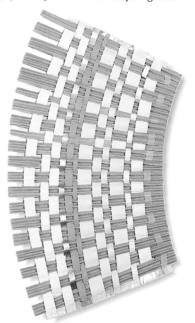

### Experimenting with shapes
*The artist has created a diversity of bas-relief forms by experimenting with folding, pleating, curling, crumpling, and twisting paper. Another technique is to laminate by gluing layers of paper together to create thicker forms, which can be carved and cut into in the manner of cardboard.*

### Tonal collage
A simple means of altering the perception of objects in a bas-relief collage is to change their natural color, or to reproduce their form in another material, such as plaster (as seen in the child's hand at the bottom of this composition). The forms, by being sprayed white, have taken on the characteristic qualities of a sculptural arrangement. In the absence of color the qualities of form and texture are amplified and produce contrasts of light and shadow.

### Working in paper
By working with paper, you can create complex bas-relief collages that explore folding, cutting, and weaving techniques. The advantage of using paper for construction is the ease with which you can fashion and glue shapes in any position. Initially, you should use neutral-toned papers, so that you will be able to see clearly and exploit the tonal play of shadows created by the folds in the paper.

### Fine details
*The forms in this composition echo landscape textures and architectural structure. The elements of wind and air are suggested by the two cross shapes that bring to mind the blades of a windmill. In this complex work, the artist explores the illusion of space by over lapping the forms to create the sensation of recession.*

57

# GALLERY OF COLLAGE

COLLAGE IS AN ESSENTIALLY modern technique. Its unique feature is that it allows artists to explore arrangements of printed materials and found objects as ready-made imagery. By composing these items into harmonious arrangements and unlikely juxtapositions, artists challenge our perception of the familiar and create a new visual language.

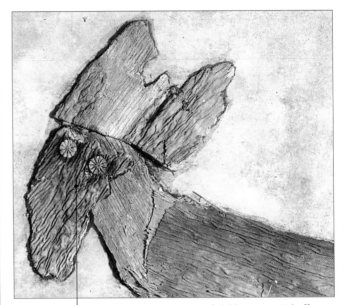

**In this deliberate** pastiche of children's art, Dubuffet has combined the complex, natural texture of dried leaves with a quirky use of imagery in the form of a stray donkey. There is no attempt to force the material to look like the subject; rather he relies on the title to prompt an imaginative reading of the materials.

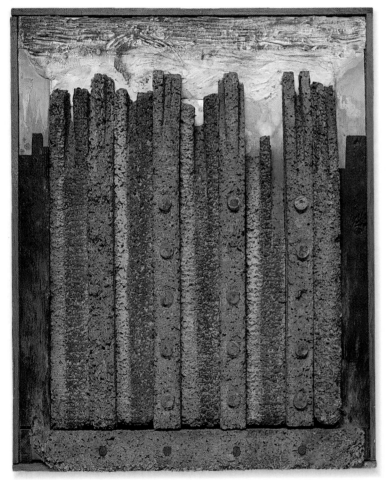

**Max Ernst, *Dadaville*, 1924, painted plaster and cork on canvas**
*26 x 22 in (66 x 56 cm)*
Max Ernst's (1891–1976) collage work is characterized by the diversity of found materials. As a soldier in World War I he was radically affected by the absurd waste and destruction he witnessed. This led to a profound skepticism about the establishment in life and art. In this work, Ernst creates an illusion of city structure by juxtaposing and transforming found materials into an arrangement with new meaning.

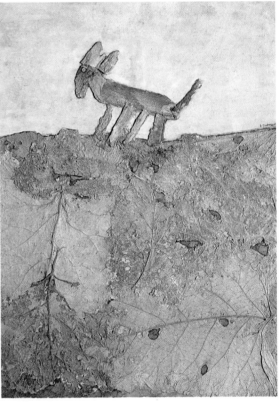

**Jean Dubuffet, *L'âne égaré*, 1959, leaves and bark** *27 x 20 in (68 x 51 cm)*
*Jean Dubuffet trained as a painter, but he is also noted for his unconventional use of materials in the creation of "Art Brut" (raw art) imagery. Dubuffet experimented extensively with heavily textured surfaces by adding sand to paint and collaging with found materials. He would use textures as diverse as printed images and butterfly wings. The artist deliberately combines contradictory qualities, bringing together an esthetically refined and subtle control of texture.*

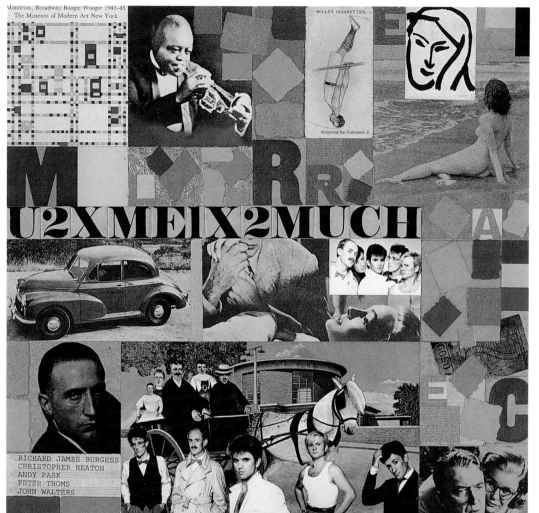

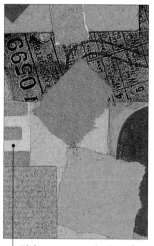

**Peter Blake, CBE, RA**
*Manhattan Boogie Woogie,*
**1994 photo-collage**
*12½ x 12½ in (32 x 32 cm)*
*Along with David Hockney and Richard Hamilton, Peter Blake was a key figure in the Pop Art movement. His originality lies in the deliberate use of the transient imagery of advertising and mass culture that had previously been regarded as outside the bounds of fine art.*

**Blake creates a** rhythm of negative shapes, produced by a deliberate arrangement of cut forms, using only found imagery.

**Anneli Boon,**
*Untitled,* **1994, paper,**
**photocopies and**
**emulsion paint**
*18 x 13 in  (45 x 33 cm)*
*Anneli Boon has used photographs of architectural forms that have then been reproduced using a photocopier. The modern process of photocopying, with its additional facilities for enlarging and reducing the scale of the image, produces a large range of material for the artist. Here, several copies of the same image, in different ratios of scale, have been cut out and then pasted onto a textured sheet of paper that has been distressed by staining and crumpling the surface.*

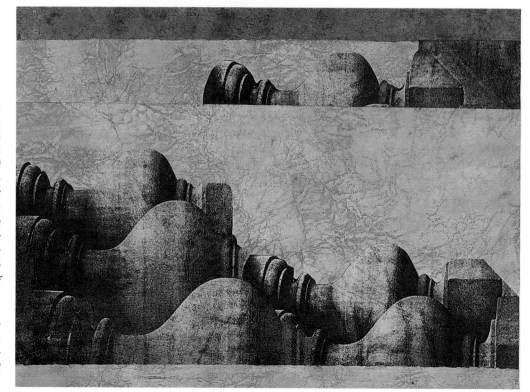

59

# Block Printmaking

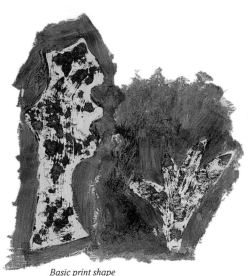

*Basic print shape*

Block printmaking is a technique of relief printing that involves cutting a design into a block. Traditionally, wood blocks and linoleum are used, but there is a wide selection of alternative materials that can be carved or cut into without using carving chisels. A sharp craft knife can be used to carve printing blocks from thick sheets of cardboard, root vegetables, erasers, polystyrene, and plaster of paris. Where the surface of the block has been cut away, the ink will not be absorbed and the area will appear as white in the final printed image.

*Basic print shape*

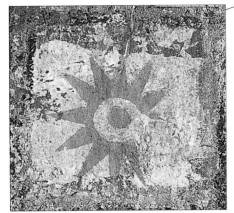

*Cardboard cutouts to use as printing shapes*

The simplest way to block print is to cut shapes out of a thick piece of cardboard, paint them with a water-based paint, and press the cardboard, paint side down, onto a sheet of paper. Making a print using small blocks involves pressing the block onto a pad of printing ink or brushing paint onto the raised surface of the block. The block is then positioned and pressed onto the paper, leaving a print of its cut shape. You can create

### Using found prints

Block printing is an excellent technique to use in combination with collage. Here the artist has used a combination of media with a selection of found materials. A sheet of brown paper has been treated with a broken application of white paint to create a surface suggesting a weathered wall. Sections of printed materials, including musical manuscripts and images of palmists' hands, have been incorporated into the printwork.

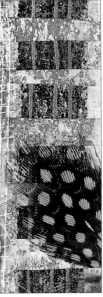

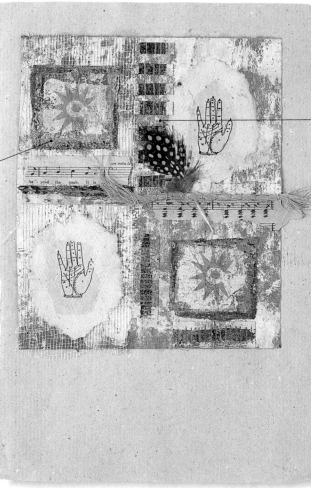

**The artist has built** up this design in a limited color range to focus our attention on the rich variety of textures in the work. The gold border has been printed from an eraser cut into the shape of a star. The gold paint has been applied to the handmade block and carefully repeated diagonally across the composition.

**A sheet of** brown paper was textured with white gouache using a sponge. The artist then collaged sections of a musical score, hand-painted strips of paper, gauze, string, and feathers to contrast with the underlying texture of the paper.

**Flea Cooke,** *Ancient Signs*, 1993, **Collage and prints**

### Dream garden

This composition was developed using broad applications of violet, green, and yellow ink to evoke the images and colors of a garden. The pattern of parallel lines, evocative of garden fencing, were produced by bleaching out the ink using a fine brush.

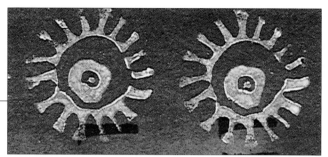

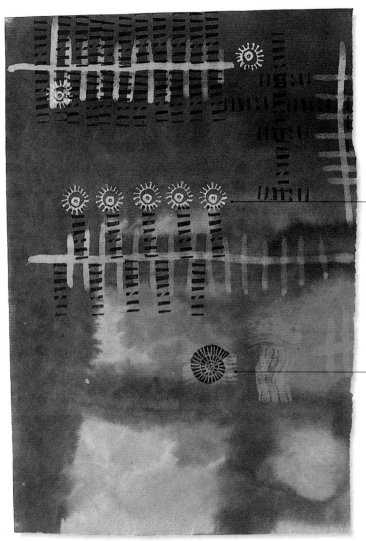

**The pressure of the print** block squeezes the paint towards the edges of the cut shape. As a result, the printed shape will look slightly transparent and will have a distinct raised edge of opaque color.

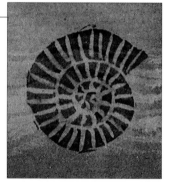

**The isolated location** of this single block print (representing a snail) has given the composition a point of focus away from the repetition of shapes in the upper section. The design in the block was created by cutting a spiral line, then superimposing a series of lines radiating from the center of the shape.

**Flea Cooke, *The garden*, 1993, block printing and bleach**

a repeat print using this method by reinking and applying the same block several times to create a recurring pattern. In the case of larger block prints, the block is inked with a roller, which will apply the ink evenly to the raised surface of the block. A sheet of smooth paper is carefully placed on the inked surface, and even pressure should then be applied to the surface of the paper to lift an impression onto the paper. Pressure can be applied by either using a roller or rubbing the back of a large wooden spoon across the back of the paper. It is neccessary to stop at intervals while rubbing and lift one corner of the paper at a time to check that the rubbing has evenly lifted the ink onto the paper.

## EASY-TO-MAKE BLOCKS FOR PRINTING

This selection of small blocks are all carved from plastic erasers. The erasers had a design drawn in ballpoint pen, and the negative shapes were cut away using a craft knife. You can either press the cut block onto an inked printing pad or use a brush to apply paint to the raised areas of the block. Delightful repeat patterns can be created by reinking and printing the same block across different areas of the artwork.

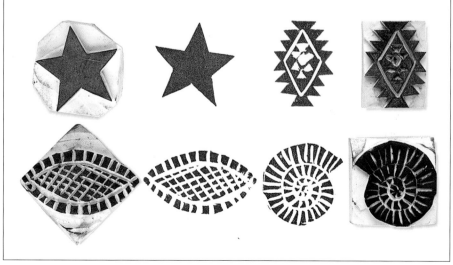

# MONOPRINT

**Materials**

*Clean sheet of glass*

*Pencil*

*Turpentine*

*Masking tape*

MONOPRINT IS A SIMPLE and manageable printmaking technique that gives exciting results particularly in the texture of the printed surface. It is so named because it is a method of printing that produces a single print from a smooth sheet of metal, glass, or acetate, any of which can be used as the printing plate. The plate can be worked on in a number of ways – by painting and wiping ink into a design or by using stencils to create shapes. A monotype print is an ideal base for a mixed media composition since you can overwork the print with pastels or paints.

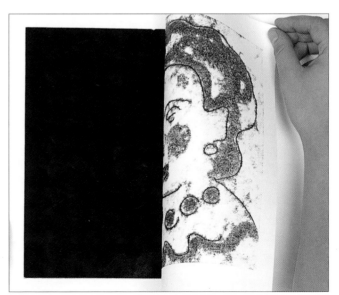

**1** ◀ To ink the roller, squeeze a line of ink from the tube at the top of the plate and roll the ink so that it is evenly distributed over the plate.

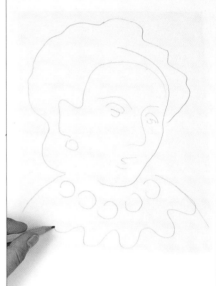

**2** ▶ Place a sheet of paper onto the plate, avoiding movement. Draw a design onto the paper using a pencil. Avoid touching the paper with your hand.

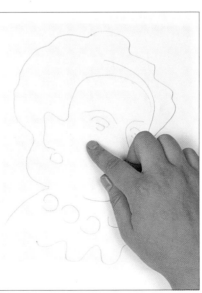

**3** ◀ You can create areas of tone by gently pressing your finger onto the back of the paper. This will lift ink from the plate onto the paper surface.

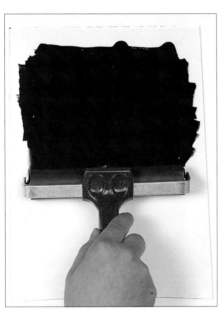

**4** ▶ Again, being careful not to touch the back of the paper, in contact with the plate, lift the paper from the plate by pulling away from one corner. The print will be a mirror image of the original drawing.

## Alternative method

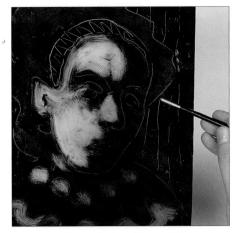

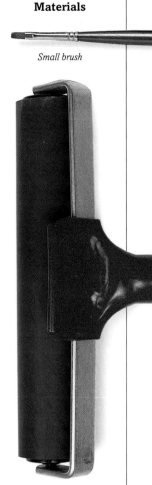

*Small brush*

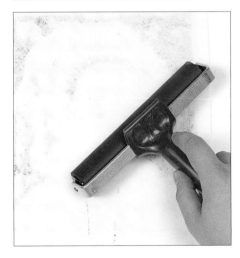

1 ▲ Another technique is to roll ink onto the plate and then wipe and scrape lines into the ink to create areas of white.

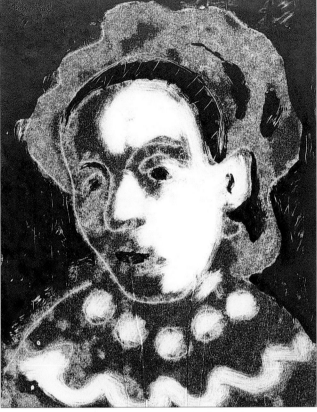

2 ◀ Place a large sheet of paper on the plate, and tape down securely. Use a roller to apply pressure and lift the image from the plate.

3 ▲ In the final print, you can see how the details, added using a fine brush with diluted ink, create a striking positive and negative tonal image.

*Rubber roller*

*Tubes of ink*

*Any suitable paper*

---

### USING STENCILS AND OVERWORKING

Monoprints can be developed into sophisticated images by building up the print using stencils. A shape is drawn onto a sheeet of paper or cardboard and cut out. The printing plate is then inked in the normal way and the paper stencil laid on the plate. The stencil masks out areas of the plate, and when the printing paper is placed and the impression is lifted off, the stencil shape remains untouched by the ink. By using stencils of different shapes, a complex design of superimposed shapes can be built up into a multilayered print. Once a monoprint has been produced you can overwork the basic shapes with pastels, paint, or crayons.

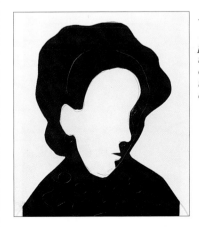

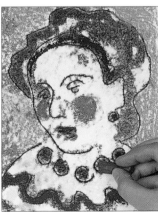

1 *The plate was inked and two stencils were applied to the plate – one for the silhouette of the figure and one for the shape of the face. Lines were inscribed into areas of ink to add detail and then a print was lifted.*

2 *The finished print can be worked on in a range of mixed media. You can overwork the print with soft pastel to add color or even watercolor that will be resisted by the oil-based ink.*

# COLLAGRAPH PRINTING

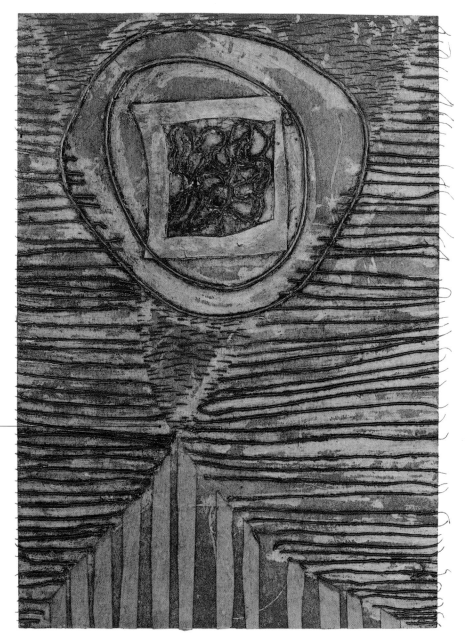

COLLAGRAPH IS A PRINTING TECHNIQUE that involves building up, rather than cutting away, a bas-relief surface. The name collagraph is a derivative of collage, as a collagraph is a technique of collaging materials to create a print. A bas-relief design is created by gluing materials to a stiff sheet of cardboard. A great variety of textured materials can be used, from coarse cloth, sand, and string to grasses and grains. The textured collagraph produces a print with an embossed surface that mirrors the bas-relief surface of the original collagraph.

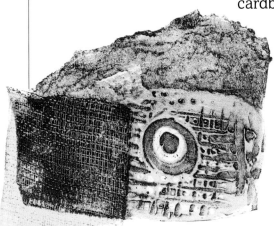

*Collagraphs can be displayed as works of art in their own right.*

*String*

## Basic collagraph

In this collagraph a sheet of stiff cardboard has been used as a base for an interesting diversity of bas-relief textures. A pattern has been created by gluing string to the surface to form a linear design. Using a craft knife a pattern of marks has been scored into the cardboard and other shapes cut from paper to create contrasting areas of texture. A collagraph can also be constructed purely from PVA glue by dribbling the glue across the cardboard or by laying down a thick area of glue and drawing into the wet surface to create negative lines.

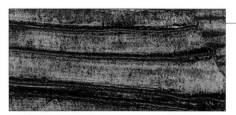

**In this composition** a linear design has been created by using string, and additional textures have been produced by cutting into the cardboard. A unique feature of collagraph printing is that the collagraph itself acquires a subtle beauty by being constantly inked, wiped, and reinked in different colors. Many collagraphs are kept and framed as bas-relief works.

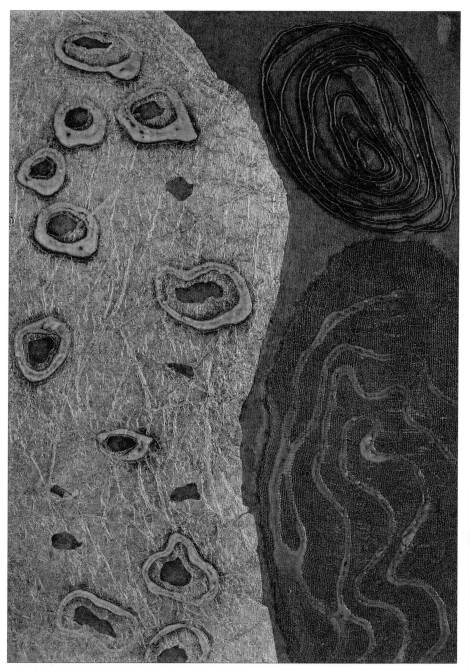

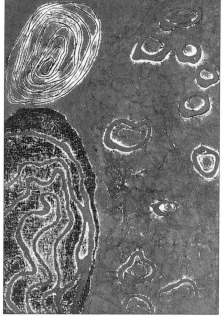

**Monotone print**

*In this first print taken from the original collagraph (see left), there is a surprisingly different appearance. The artist used a roller to ink the collagraph in a single dark blue color. The raised surface of the materials has created a striking white halo around the textured forms in the print.*

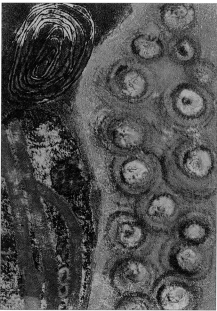

**Multicolored print**

*In this second impression from the same collagraph, the composition is radically altered by the application of different colors. The artist has carefully painted different colors on various parts of the print to create two contrasting halves to the composition and to amplify the circular forms.*

To BUILD UP up a collagraph, you can use many materials, including wallpaper, fine and coarse cloths, netting, and light metals such as foil. When the design is finished the surface should be sealed with PVA glue or shellac. After the surface has dried the collagraph is inked using a roller or a brush. A sheet of paper is laid face down on the print and the back of the paper rubbed in the same manner as block printing. If you dampen the surface of the paper it will accept the ink more readily.

**Original collagraph**

Anneli Boon is a Finnish artist who has explored the patterns in the strata of weathered rock formations as a source for her collagraph compositions. She has created this collagraph using a combination of fine gauze, a sheet of foil, string, and dribbled glue. The design was painted over in a coat of shellac to seal the surface, allowed to dry, and inked using a roller. A sheet of paper was laid on the print and held in place with masking tape. The back of the paper was then rubbed to lift an impression from the collagraph.

# GALLERY OF MONOPRINT

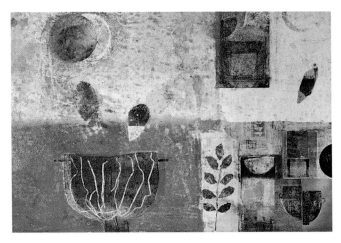

THE SIMPLE TECHNIQUE of monoprint has been used by these artists to create a remarkably diverse range of visual imagery, from monochrome prints that have the quality of tonal drawing to complex multilayered color compositions. Printmaking is normally associated with multiple editions of the same image. However, monoprint, as the name implies, involves building up a single print surface and in this sense is closer to the process of creating a painting. Monoprints can be produced either by transferring a painting on a plate to paper or by using a roller to impart a uniform texture onto the printed image. Artists who work in monoprint frequently overwork the print using paints or pastels.

**Tom Wood,** *Monoprint II,* **1991, monoprint**
*42 x 63½ in (106.5 x 160.5 cm)*
*Tom Wood has developed a complex surface of overlaid colors in a monoprint based on a still life. The surface of the print has been built up through multiple layers of colored ink. Cut paper stencils were used to mask areas of the plate, creating the shapes within the composition.*

**The artist has cut** leaf shapes out of paper and laid them onto the printed surface of the paper. Where these stencil shapes have been applied to the print, the subsequent application of white ink has been masked from the paper. The stencil was then pulled away from the paper, revealing the color and texture of the previous layer of ink.

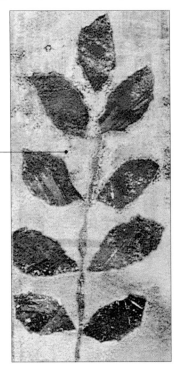

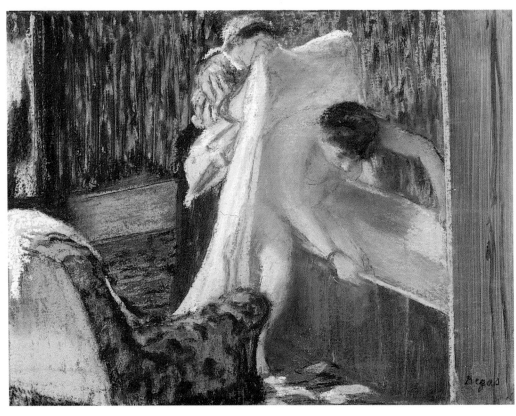

**Edgar Degas,** *Woman Leaving Her Bath,* **1876–77, monotype and pastel**
*6¼ x 8½ in (16 x 21.5 cm)*
*Degas was a master draftsman who obsessively explored the theme of the body in movement. He contributed greatly to the development of monoprint. Here the image has been developed by brushing and wiping black ink onto a plate, and this can be seen in the gray areas of the wall. The print was overworked in pastel to add color and more texture.*

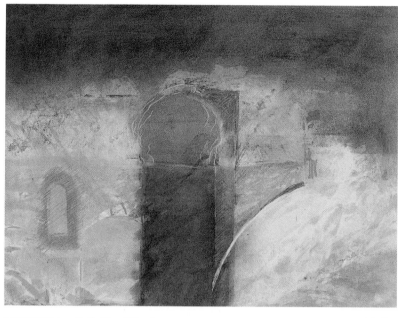

**Bob Baggaley,** *Avebury Rd,* **1993, monotype**
*16 x 20 in (40.5 x 51 cm)*
*Bob Baggaley combines different print processes to create monoprints based on a landscape theme. An image is printed using either silkscreen or lithography, and individual prints are then overworked using a monoprint process. The artist has experimented with the surface by dissolving the top layer of the ink with a thinner to reveal the previous layers of color.*

**Bill Jacklin, RA,** *Untitled,* **1993, monotype**
*40 x 48 in (101.5 x 121.5 cm)*
*In this energetic monoprint of figures bathing, the artist has used the pronounced texture of sweeping brushstrokes in blue and green ink to evoke the motion of the waves. He then dropped thinner onto the plate in spots to displace the ink and create the effect of foam. A small brush has been used for the fine details of the figures in motion.*

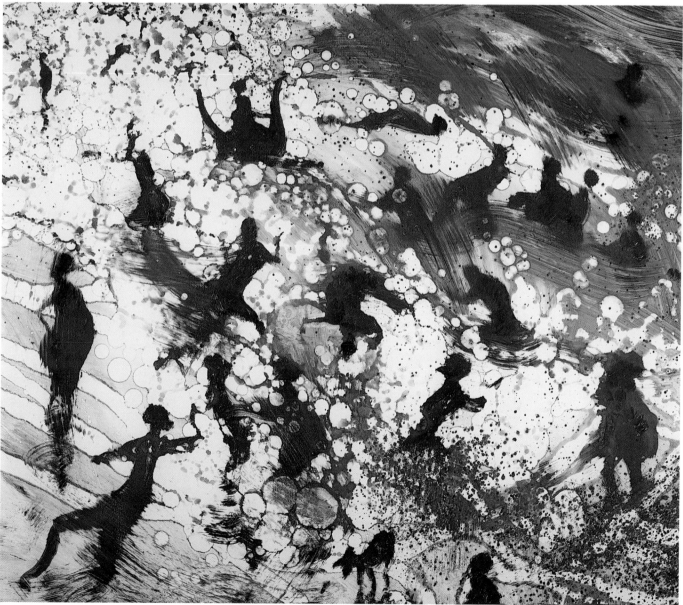

# PRESERVING AND STORING

PRESERVING AND STORING finished works requires careful consideration since mixed media surfaces are easily spoiled by careless handling. Framing under glass is the best solution for preserving bas-relief work, because this isolates the artwork's surface from air pollution. Works can also be stored in a portfolio with a covering sheet of tissue paper.

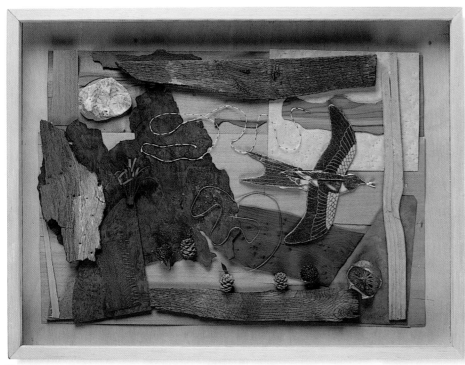

**Box frame**
*In this assemblage a box frame has been specifically designed to provide adequate clearance for the different elements that make up the bas-relief. This type of framing enables the irregular format of the composition to be seen clearly and gives the artwork a more interesting perspective.*

THE BEST METHOD FOR preserving your work depends on the size of the piece and the nature of the materials used in the composition. As a general rule it is recommended that oil- and acrylic-based paintings be given a coat of picture varnish to preserve the surface of the work from airborne pollution. This is sufficient protection as it is expensive to frame large works under glass. You can store works on canvas and board by wrapping them in polyethylene or bubble wrap when transporting the work. Encaustic painting, heavily textured, and bas-relief surfaces along with collage and works on paper will absorb dust and moisture from the surrounding atmosphere. Since these surfaces are not recommended for varnishing, they are best framed under glass.

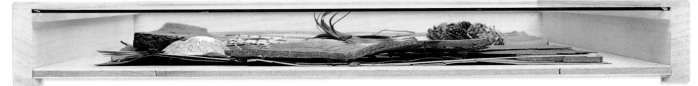

**Cross-section of the box frame**
*In this cross-sectional view of the box frame, you can see that this design of frame is deep enough to allow adequate clearance for the bas-relief forms in the composition.*

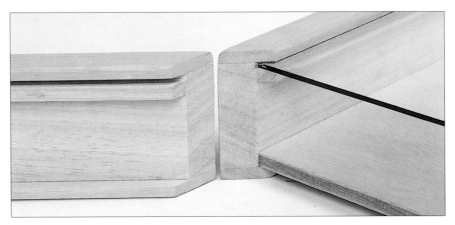

**Corner view**
*A box frame differs from other frames in that the glass and the base are held apart by slotting into recesses that are cut into the inner edge of the molding.*

## Framing under glass

There are many different frames. The best way to choose a suitable one is to visit a contemporary gallery or a professional picture framer to see the various types available. Some wooden frames have molding that is stained or coated in gesso or gilt to form a more elaborate surface. Aluminum frames can also be purchased in kits. In some cases you may need to have glass cut to size. Framing has a tremendous effect on the appearance of a work and will greatly enhance its presence and value. Choose a frame that allows for a border of at least 2-3 in (5-7 cm) around a work. Test the color of the frame against the artwork so that you can see if the color goes with the composition. Usually, works on paper are mounted on cardboard and a mat placed over the work. If you choose this method of framing it is essential that the color of the mat works with the key colors of the composition.

**Handmade frame**

*In this inventive frame scraps from a sawmill have been used to create a frame that has the particularly original feature of string linking the corners.*

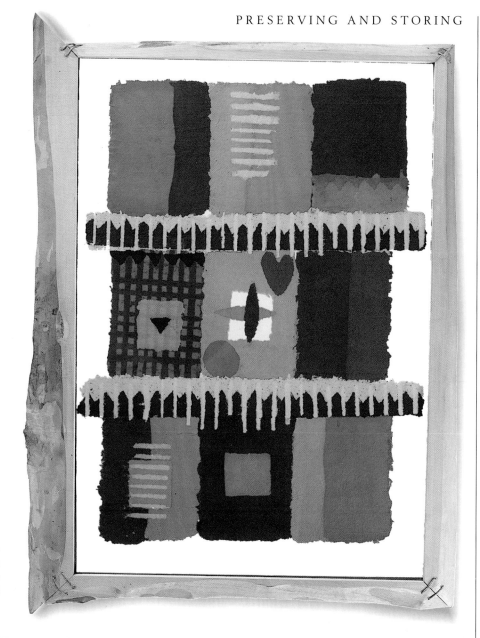

## FIXING AND STORING

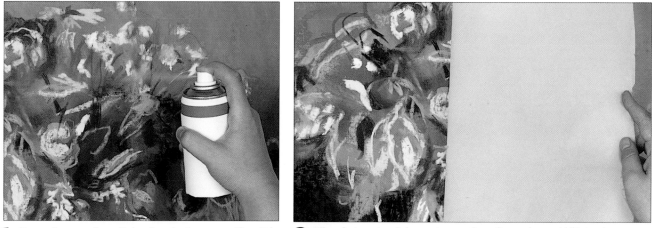

1 *Dry media are easily spoiled and need to be preserved by a light spray of fixative to fix the pigment to the support. Do not overspray the surface as this can darken or displace the pigment.*

2 *When storing artwork, be sure to cover the surface and to avoid friction that displaces the surface pigment. Make a cover by taping a sheet of tissue, greaseproof or tracing paper to a piece of cardboard and place the artwork underneath.*

# GLOSSARY

**ACRYLIC PAINTS** Are bound by an acrylic and are water-soluble but unlike watercolor and gouache, they dry to an insoluble plastic film. Acrylic is ideal for creating surface texture in a painting, since it can be worked in thick impasto or with added texturing. Manufacturers have developed a variety of additives that can be added to alter the texture of the paint or retard the drying time. This allows for more controlled blending of colors.

**ART BOARD** Artists' quality paper mounted on cardboard. It gives the support a stiffness that reduces the incidences of pastel loss caused by the flexing of the paper surface.

**ARTISTS' QUALITY PAPER** Paper with a neutral pH balance and a high rag content that does not yellow and become brittle with age.

**ARTISTS' QUALITY PAINT** These paints are labeled with information on the nature of the pigment and lightfastness of the color.

**BLENDING** A technique used in the manipulation of dry drawing and painting media such as charcoal, chalks, and pastels. Using either a finger, brush, tissue, or cloth, colors can be worked into each other on the support to achieve smooth gradations of tone.

**BLOCK PRINTING** A technique of relief printing that involves cutting a design into a block. Traditionally woodblocks or linoleum are used but there is a wide selection of other materials, such as thick sheets of cardboard, root vegetables, plastic erasers, polystyrene, and plaster of paris, which can be carved or cut using either wood-carving chisels or a sharp craft knife. The surface of the block is inked and a print taken by applying pressure to the back of a sheet of paper placed on the inked block. The areas where the surface of the block is cut away appear as white lines or negative shapes in the printed image.

**CANVAS** There are two main types of canvas: artist's linen, made from flax, and cotton duck. You can purchase preprimed canvases on stretchers of various sizes or prepare your own.

**CHARCOAL** Carbonized wood made by charring willow, vine, or other twigs in airtight containers.

**COLLAGRAPH PRINT** Collagraph is a printing technique that involves building up a bas-relief surface using light materials that are arranged and glued onto a stiff sheet of cardboard in the manner of a collage. The raised surface is inked and a print is taken by applying pressure to the back of a sheet of paper placed on the inked surface. Collagraph prints have a characteristically embossed surface that mirrors the bas-relief forms of the original materials.

**DAMMAR** A soft resin that is soluble in turpentine and used to make a gloss varnish. You can make an acceptable varnish by dissolving some dammar resin in a jar of turpentine or mineral spirits.

**DIFFUSER** A spray diffuser is a tool for spraying either a liquid pigment or fixative in atomized droplets onto the surface of a support. Two small hinged metal tubes are opened at right angles to each other with the end of the longer tube immersed in the medium. Hold the shorter end with the plastic mouth piece between your lips and blow firmly. The action of your breath will cause the fluid to rise up the longer tube and atomize the liquid into a fine spray. You can vary the density of the spray according to the pressure of your breath and the distance you hold the diffuser from the support.

**FIXATIVE** A resin dissolved in solvent that is sprayed onto a charcoal or pastel work to fix the particles of the medium to the support. Fixative is also used between layers of dry drawing and painting media to stop the previous layer from blending with the next application of color. Fixative should be used sparingly, since a heavy application will alter the appearance of the work

**FROTTAGE** A technique of taking a rubbing from a textured surface. A sheet of thin paper is placed onto the textured surface and the side or blunt end of a stick of charcoal or crayon is rubbed vigorously over the back of the paper. The crayon will impart pigment to the paper only where the raised areas of the textured surface are in contact with the paper.

**GESSO** A primer manufactured for creating bas-relief and textured supports.

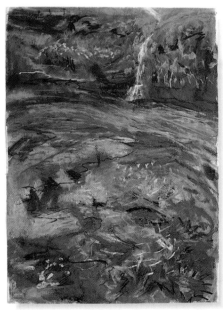

*Waterfall study*

*Pastels*

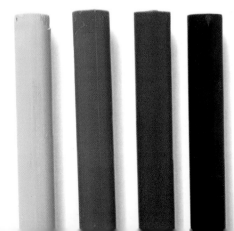

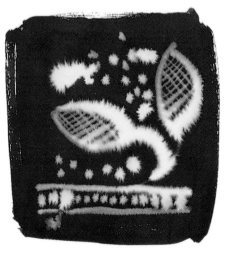

*Bleach and ink*

**IMPASTO** A dense application of paint that forms a bas-relief surface.

**INKS** The main types are water-based and shellac-based inks. Shellac inks are water-proof when dry and are suitable for overpainting.

**KNEADED ERASERS** These are suitable for erasing a range of dry drawing media such as pencil, charcoal, chalk, and pastel. The particular quality of the kneaded erasers is that the medium's particles adhere to the eraser and are lifted from the fibers of the paper when it is pressed against the surface of a drawing. These erasers can be kneaded into a fine point for detailed work, where you can effectively use them as a drawing tool, creating highlights in your work as you remove the pigment and reveal the surface below.

**LAMINATING** An extension of collage. It is a process of gluing thin sheets of tissue paper over each other between layers of PVA (polyvinyl acetate) glue. The glue transforms the tissue paper into transparent sheets of color.

**MASKING FLUID** This is a latex liquid that can be applied with a brush or dip pen to mask out areas of an artwork before applying another wash.

**MASKING OUT** A technique of covering areas of the support using either masking tape or a sheet of paper to block a subsequent application of medium. After applying the medium, the masking tape or sheet is removed to reveal the previous tone of the support that shows through the application of medium.

**MONOPRINT** A printing technique that results in a single print.

**MONOTYPE** A form of monoprint that involves applying ink to a plate in a design and taking a print. The process of inking the plate can be repeated and applied to the same paper so that an image is built up in layers. Stencils cut from paper can be used to mask out areas and create shapes in the design of the print.

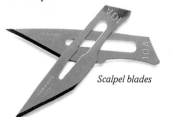
*Scalpel blades*

**OIL PAINT** Paint bound by poppy or linseed oil. It is the most popular medium for easel painting because of its ease of manipulation and saturated colors. With the addition of resin such as dammar varnish or gel medium, it is possible to glaze washes of color in oil paint.

**OIL PASTEL** Pastel bound by oil as opposed to gum. The oil gives it a slight transparency and a strong adherence to the support. There are fewer colors available than in soft pastels.

**OPTICAL MIX** This occurs when small areas of colors next to each other appear to the eye, at a certain distance, to merge and become a third color – red and yellow dots will mix and become orange.

**PVA** Polyvinyl acetate is a glue medium used for gluing paper and binding pigments to the surface of the support.

**SGRAFFITO** The technique of scratching lines in a surface application of color using a blunted knife. The lines reveal the original surface color of the support which contrasts with the application of the overlaid color.

**SCUMBLING** A technique of layering colors by means of a light application of the side of a pastel, which allows some of the support or previous application of pastel to show through the new application of color.

**SOFT PASTELS** The original form of pastel manufactured in the widest range of up to three hundred colors and tints. Pigments are mixed with a light solution of gum tragacanth and precipitated chalk to

*Pastel frottage*

create the tints of colors. The weak solution of gum ensures a very soft texture making this form of pastel most suitable for painting techniques.

**STIPPLING** The technique of applying colors in small points using a stabbing and dotting application of the tip of a pastel.

**SUPPORT** The surface you choose, for example, paper, board, or canvas.

**TOOTH OF PAPER** Paper, when examined under a microscope, appears as a felted weave of fibers, which trap the particles of color from a dry medium. The coarser the texture of the paper, the more tooth and the more medium is retained by the paper surface.

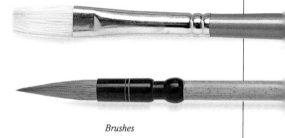
*Brushes*

**WAX ENCAUSTIC** A painting medium made by mixing powdered pigments into melted beeswax. The advantage of wax is that it is a very stable coloring medium – it does not darken with age in the manner of oil paint. It is more complicated to use because, to keep the medium in a liquid state, the pigment is manipulated using heat. The melted wax can also be thinned to a maleable paste by adding turpentine. When the mixture is set, it is mixed with oil paint.

---

A NOTE ON TOXICITY

• When using and combining a wide selection of materials it is important to be aware of the health hazards.

All art materials are required by law to label clearly their chemical contents and levels of toxicity. You should avoid inhaling the dust from powder pigments and fumes from thinners, glues, and fixative sprays. It is also important to be aware that pigments and thinners can be absorbed through the skin; therefore prolonged contact should be avoided. Always keep the lids of solvent jars screwed on tight and only use as much as you need at any one time. Artists should also make sure they avoid licking brushes with paint on them. If you are in any doubt about the toxicity of a product, contact the manufacturer directly.

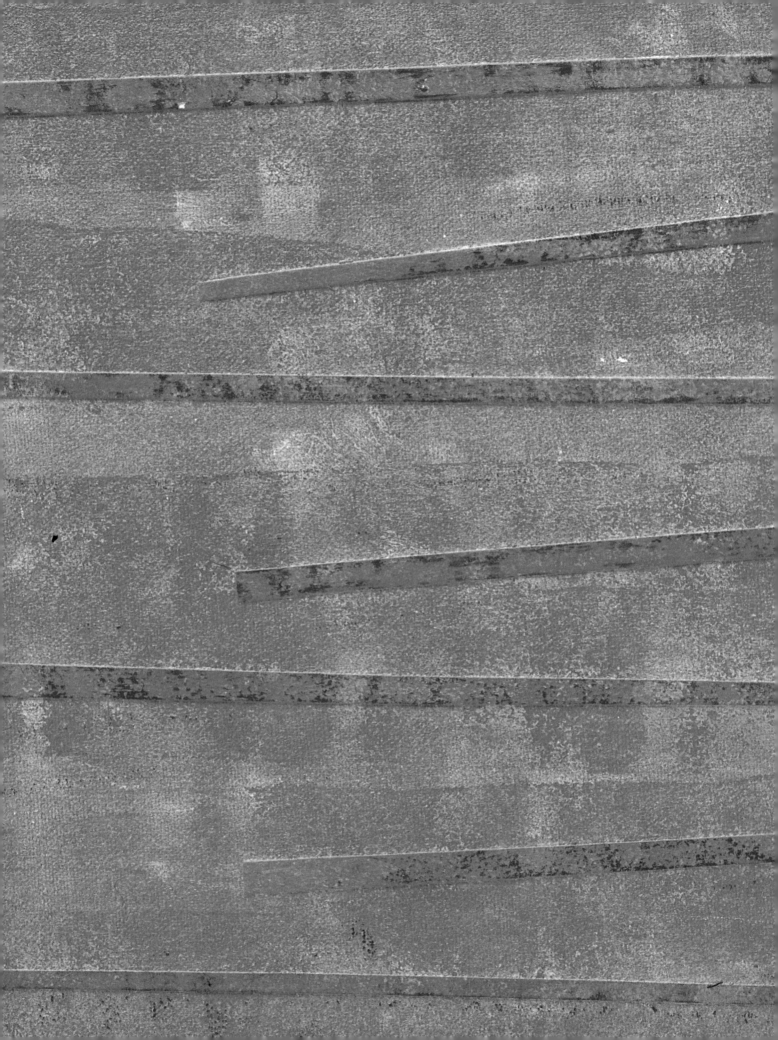